PROTESTANT-CATHOLIC MARRIAGES
CAN SUCCEED

Protestant-Catholic Marriages Can Succeed

By *PAUL and* JEANNE SIMON

Paul Simon

ASSOCIATION PRESS
NEW YORK

Dedicated to our children
Sheila and Martin

"The greatest changes within human life thus come to pass when a man has awakened to the existence of his brethren. And when we come to think of our own times, we must take heart that such an awakening actually is occurring all around us, in the most unexpected places . . ."

—Rev. Daniel Berrigan, S.J.
in *They Call Us Dead Men*

Foreword

This book is not to promote "mixed marriages" within the Christian family. The studies it cites show clearly that marriages between Catholics and Protestants are occurring with increasing frequency in our pluralistic culture without the aid of any promotional efforts. In fact, this increasing frequency has been occurring for some years despite all the warnings and objections of families and of the religious establishment.

Since more and more men and women are uniting in Catholic-Protestant marriages, and their families, friends, and spiritual advisers are involved with them in varying degrees, Paul and Jeanne Simon offer their own experience, enriched by careful study, as a testimony to the fact that God's call to marriage can transcend the institutional divisions within the Church. Those who respond to that call become one in His Love and by His Grace are enabled to sustain and enrich their marriage.

They call attention to the study of the World Council of Churches on "Marriage in a Divided Church" and remind us that the present situation reflects much less on those who marry across the division than it does on the responsibility of all Christians for permitting division to exist in the one Church of Jesus Christ.

Paul and Jeanne Simon have written with informed minds, carefully reporting the existing research data as well as sharing their own contemplation and reflection after almost seven years of marriage. They have written with sensitive consciences, careful to acknowledge their debts to their respective traditions, but daring to explore beyond the answers that have traditionally been given up to this time.

Most of all, the Simons write out of a deep love which they acknowledge as a gift from God. Their tenderness toward each other, toward their children, and toward all those who are wrestling with these problems is clearly evident. Their righteous indignation is reserved for the theological obscurantist or the ecclesiastical bureaucrats who would subjugate the possibilities of growth in love to the rigidities of outmoded systems and institutions.

Basically, this is a warm and personal account of how one couple is facing up to a very human situation. Not all of their solutions will satisfy every reader. Their theology has been called simplistic and some of their personal decisions are obviously beyond the limits of present Church teaching. Not all readers will be able to agree with them; some may be offended.

It is important to recognize, however, that their account comes at a time when a spirit of inquiry and change is in the air. Long-held doctrines are being re-examined and equally long-held prejudices and stereotypes are being exposed as uncouth for an ecumenical age. As our respective communities of faith draw closer to their one God and Father, we find ourselves drawn closer to each other.

Perhaps it will become clearer that the real "mixed marriage" is not between two followers of Christ but between the Christian and the nonbeliever. Even in this latter instance, however, Christians should be challenged to reach over their institutional walls to minister to persons and to do all in their power to stabilize and enrich these marriages and families.

We believe this personal testimony makes two important contributions:

It contributes knowledge of human experience to the ecumenical dialogue that is now taking place; and

It ministers to those who are involved in marriages that transcend our present institutional divisions and to the families, friends, and spiritual advisers related to such marriages. By helping all of these persons to see the problems clearly and in perspective and by helping them see the possibilities of a deep personal commitment, this book can witness to the relevancy of our Christian Gospel in this very human situation.

For these reasons, we are happy to commend the book in the unity and hope that only Christ can give.

Rev. William H. Genné
Commission on Marriage and Family
National Council of Churches

Rev. John L. Thomas, S.J.
Center for Social Studies
Cambridge, Massachusetts

A Personal Preface

Since we shall be talking about one of the most important decisions you will make or have made in your lives, you have a right to know a little about us.

We are both active members of our churches, Jeanne a Roman Catholic and Paul a Lutheran. We have been married almost seven years as this is written—long enough to know some of the problems of marriage, and recently enough to remember some of the pangs and heartache we went through prior to our wedding day because of our differing religious affiliations and convictions.

Both of us were members of the Illinois House of Representatives when we first met. Both of us were single—and it was *not* "love at first sight." We met in 1956 and were married in 1960. After we were well acquainted, before we even dated each other, Paul said to friends who jokingly asked him about his marital status that he was waiting for a "Lutheran Jeanne Hurley" and Jeanne said she was waiting for a "Catholic Paul Simon."

We slowly came to the decision that despite all the advice we were getting we should get married.

Temporarily this meant severing some ties. Paul felt he should resign from a national Lutheran youth board on which he served, and he was somewhat awkwardly dropped from another national Luthern committee, which suddenly felt a little defiled by a member who would go contrary to so much church teaching and marry a Catholic. Jeanne moved from Wilmette to Troy, and this meant leaving the board of directors of a diocesan group with which she had worked.

But neither of us left our basic moorings. Today Paul is on more committees of the Lutheran church nationally than ever and teaches a Sunday-school class at St. Paul's Lutheran Church in Troy. Jeanne is an officer of the regional deanery, in addition to being chairman of the parish confraternity board and one of the more active members of St. Jerome's Catholic Church here in Troy.

We have two happy, healthy children, for which we are most thankful.

In those agonizing months prior to our engagement and marriage we devoured everything we could read on Protestant-Catholic marriages. We felt almost all of it was negative, carping, and unduly partisan. Too many authors in both camps wrote on this subject as a chance to denounce the weaknesses of the other side, as a chance to pour out some theological vitriol while at the same time they announced boldly that they approached the problem objectively. There was little of substance to help people in our situation.

And that is why we have prepared this book.

We have not written to please either Protestant or Roman Catholic theologians; we expect there will be some criticism from both. To do a job that needs doing means stepping on some toes in both camps of Christendom.

Persons entering a Christian-Jewish or some type of mixed-faith marriage may find some points in the book which will be helpful, but it is primarily designed for the more specific audience, those considering or in a Protestant-Catholic marriage. Its implied theology applies only to this situation.

We are grateful to the following for taking the time to look at the manuscript and offer their suggestions: Father Gregory Baum, Msgr. Daniel Cantwell, Mr. and Mrs. Pat Crowley, Dr. George Lindbeck, Dr. Martin E. Marty, Mr. and Mrs. Robert McCabe, Rev. Arthur Simon, Rev. Maurice Winn, Rev. Elmer Witt.

Their kindnesses have improved the final product, but the views expressed are not necessarily theirs.

We know that more and more young people are facing the problems we faced and are facing. It is our hope that the words which follow may help you face your future realistically—and with hope.

Paul and Jeanne Simon

Troy, Illinois

Contents

Foreword   9

Preface   13

I   CHANGE IS IN THE WIND   21

Trends in Protestant-Catholic Marriage
A New Climate Is Being Established
Theology and Unity

II   THERE ARE PROBLEMS, BUT . . .   34

What Surveys Show
Desertion and Unhappiness

III   THE WRONG SOLUTION: INDIFFERENCE   42

Areas of Agreement
Avoiding Religious Indifference

IV   LEARN WHAT YOU SHARE AND SHARE WHAT YOU CAN   52

Discussion and Reading
Worship
Common Action

V   DON'T BE HARD ON YOUR RELATIVES   63

Opportunities for Understanding

VI   YOUR HOME   69

Areas for Compromise

VII   YOUR CHILDREN   76
> Knotty Problems
> Two Guides for Decision
> Explaining to Children
> Religion in the Home
> Adoption

VIII   BIRTH CONTROL   90
> Types of Problems
> Gradual Change

IX   BE WILLING TO HELP   98
> Helping Others Understand

X   A POSTSCRIPT TO THE CHURCHES   103
> Suggestions for Improvement

Appendix: Prayers Acceptable to Protestants
and Catholics   117
> The Lord's Prayer
> Table Prayer
> Night Prayers for Children
> Informal Prayers:
>> Prayer of St. Francis of Assisi
>> Morning Prayer of Martin Luther
> Prayer for Forgiveness
> Prayer After Holy Communion and
>> Other Occasions
> Prayer for Today
> Prayer for Our Marriage

PROTESTANT-CATHOLIC MARRIAGES
CAN SUCCEED

I

Change Is in the Wind

One of the Catholic canons states: "Everywhere and with the greatest strictness the church forbids marriages between baptized persons, one of whom is a Catholic and the other a member of a schismatical or heretical sect." A Lutheran publication of more recent origin, in most intemperate language, berates those who enter marriage with a Roman Catholic, "condemning unborn children to the soul-destroying religion of the anti-Christ."

A host of similar quotations can be obtained from both Roman Catholic and Protestant* sources.

Despite all these protestations by church leaders, Protestant-Catholic marriages are increasing.

In recent years there has been at least a slight moderation of former positions. Pope Paul VI has announced that Catholics who marry in a non-Roman church are not

* The term "Protestant" includes so many variations, including those with virtually no beliefs, that the authors are simply assuming that the term as used in this book will be understood as describing the vast majority of those who use the name and who accept the divinity of Jesus Christ, the reality of the Trinity, and the hope of the Resurrection.

automatically excommunicated. Father Hans Kueng, prominent Catholic theologian, has joined cardinals and bishops in urging that the Vatican recognize the validity of "mixed marriages" in non-Catholic churches and that parents be given full freedom to determine the religious instruction of their children. Protestant publications are gradually less and less polemic in their exhortations to avoid a "mixed marriage"—a phrase we dislike—and call for greater study of the Catholic approach to marriage as a sacrament and as indissoluble.

In any survey of the current situation two things are apparent to the most casual observer:

1. Despite all the preachments and pronouncements, Protestant-Catholic marriages are growing, and every indication is that the rate of growth will increase.

2. Thanks in large part to the leadership of Pope John XXIII, we have entered a new era of understanding among Christians who worship in different churches.

Both points need elaboration.

TRENDS IN PROTESTANT-CATHOLIC MARRIAGE

Exactly how many marriages in the United States are Protestant-Catholic *intra*-Christian marriages no one knows. Each Catholic diocese keeps a record of Catholics marrying Protestants in the Catholic church. The records differ, from a heavily Catholic area—like Rhode Island— where marriages to Protestants are infrequent, to areas like some in the South where Catholics are relatively few and marriages to Protestants are in the large majority. Father John L. Thomas, former sociologist at St. Louis University, and now affiliated with the Cambridge (Massachusetts) Center for Social Studies, believes that just under one third of all Catholic marriages termed "valid" (i.e., within the Catholic church) are with Protestants.[1] A 1955 study placed the figure at 27 per cent.[2] In addition there are many Catholics who marry outside the church, this figure considerably less firm than the former. Research in Iowa showed more than twice as many Protestant-Catholic marriages recorded by the state than by the Catholic dioceses of Iowa during a five-year period, 11,593 noted by the state and 5,325 noted in church records.[3] This tends to confirm the study, which reached the conclusion that approximately one half of U.S. Roman Catholics wed Protestants. Rev. Ladislav Orsy, S.J., a Hungarian canonist in Rome, was quoted in the *St. Louis Review* as saying that in the 1950's 80 per cent of the "mixed marriages" contracted in Holland, 75 per cent in Germany and 57 per cent in Switzerland were invalid according to church law.

The trend for marriage outside of one's original moorings is also clear in Protestant churches. The Bossard-Boll study of Lutherans showed that in 1936–40, 46 per cent of Lutherans marrying did so outside their church; in 1941–45, 47 per cent; and in 1946–50, 58 per cent.[4] This study, published in 1957, showed that one out of five Lutherans marrying chose a Catholic spouse. That figure undoubtedly has risen since that time; one Protestant study finds the increase in Protestants marrying Catholics "astonishing."[5]

In the United States statistics are not kept of religious affiliation at marriage, except since 1953 in the state of Iowa. Census figures of religious affiliation are available for all married couples in the nation, but for a variety of reasons—change of church affiliation being a major one—give no real clue to the number of Protestant-Catholic marriages taking place. Canada keeps statistics on religious affiliation at marriage, but neither Canada nor Iowa is typical of the total religious make-up in the United States, so the statistics on the number of such marriages may bear little relationship to the United States national picture. Iowa, for example, is 16 per cent Catholic compared to 26 per cent for the nation. Both Iowa and Canada are more rural than is the general United States population; since other studies show that the rate of Protestant-Catholic marriages is higher in the United States in urban and suburban areas, it can be presumed that the rate is lower in Iowa and Canada than for the general United States population. However, the trend observable in the Canadian marriages, which unfortunately cannot be so precisely documented in the United States, is valid in both countries—and probably also in the Netherlands, Germany, and other nations with a population of mixed religious backgrounds.

Here are statistics from a few years based on figures provided by the Canadian government: [6]

Table I

Percentage of Roman Catholic Grooms Marrying Protestants

1931	8.7	1961	12.0
1941	9.7	1962	12.1
1951	10.8	1963	12.5
1956	11.2		

Table II

Percentage of Roman Catholic Brides Marrying Protestants

1931	10.9	1961	12.8
1941	12.1	1962	12.9
1951	11.8	1963	13.4
1956	12.3		

If the same figures were available for the United States, while the percentage of Catholics marrying Protestants would be much higher, the basic trend would be the same. Even these figures can be deceptive, since a percentage figure was used. Because there were many more marriages in Canada in 1963 than in 1931, the actual number of Protestant-Catholic marriages has more than tripled, while the percentage of such marriages also has climbed steadily.

The largest Protestant body in Canada is the United Church of Canada, but since there is no exact counterpart to that group in the United States, the next two in size were taken for a similar analysis, the Anglicans—usually called Episcopalians in the United States—and the Lutherans.

Table III

Percentage of Anglican Grooms Marrying Catholics

1931	8.2	1961	12.9
1941	9.2	1962	13.1
1951	10.3	1963	13.4
1956	11.6		

Table IV

Percentage of Anglican Brides Marrying Catholics

1931	6.1	1961	12.5
1941	7.2	1962	12.8
1951	9.4	1963	13.4
1956	10.9		

For the Anglican brides the numbers are even more impressive than the percentages. In 1931 there were 9,781 Anglican brides married, 595 of them to Roman Catholics. In 1963 there were 15,471 Anglican brides married, 2,078 to Roman Catholics.

Table V

Percentage of Lutheran Grooms Marrying Catholics

1931	6.7	1961	14.9
1941	10.2	1962	16.0
1951	11.4	1963	16.4
1956	14.2		

Numerically this represents a growth from 219 out of 3,252 in 1931 to 830 out of 5,045 in 1963.

Table VI

Percentage of Lutheran Brides Marrying Catholics

1931	5.7	1961	9.3
1941	8.3	1962	15.9
1951	11.8	1963	15.2
1956	15.1		

While 1961 went contrary to the general trend, the pattern is nevertheless clear. Numerically this represents an increase from 179 of 3,128 marriages in 1931 to 690 of 4,542 in 1963.

These figures from Canada simply confirm the trend observable in the United States. Middle-class suburbs have the greatest percentage of Protestant-Catholic marriages, and as the United States becomes more suburban and more middle-class, the numbers and rate of Protestant-Catholic marriages also grow. Within the United States a conservative estimate is that one of five marriages is between a Protestant and a Roman Catholic, based on the limited studies which are available.

Whatever the exact figure may be, everyone admits it is growing, and all the exhortations to stop the trend by both Catholics and Protestants seem to have had little effect.

A NEW CLIMATE IS BEING ESTABLISHED

It is the belief of the authors of this book that during the years ahead Protestant-Catholic marriages will increase, rather than diminish, in part because of the new climate which is being established between the two branches of Christendom.

If Catholics and Protestants really are fellow Christians

—which we seem to be reluctantly recognizing—then it cannot be quite the evil once imagined to marry one another; that very roughly is the reasoning which more and more of marriageable age are likely to follow.

The trend toward greater understanding can hardly be denied, even though in some communities and neighborhoods the priest and pastor still hardly recognize each other. We still need to live in the present more than the past, to heed the advice of *Commonweal:* "At some point the Protestant must be able to stop looking at Pope John XXIII as if he were Alexander VI; at some point the Catholic must be able to stop looking at the local Protestant pastor as if he were a rebellious monk; at some point the Jew must be able to look at an American Cardinal without seeing an Orthodox Bishop from Czarist Russia. To know that history has left us all with scars and that these scars are often sensitive is one thing; to open up old wounds needlessly is something else again."[7]

More and more the past is being viewed by both sides with understanding, with the knowledge that all of us share guilt for the needless wars and petty bickerings which have taken place.

In this new era an excommunication of Orthodox Patriarch Michael Cerularius, which took place in 1054, has been lifted, and one of the most prominent Catholic theologians has publicly suggested that the decree of excommunication against Martin Luther also be lifted.

In St. Louis, Cardinal Ritter speaks at the commencement of the United Church of Christ's Eden Theological Seminary; and at the St. Louis Cathedral (Roman Catholic) hundreds of Catholic and Protestant clergymen join in a service, with the sermon delivered by Episcopal Bishop George L. Cadigan.

Newspaper headlines tell us of things no one would have guessed possible a decade ago: "Catholic Priest Reads Litany in Episcopal Ordination"; "Lutherans, Roman Catholics Find Agreement on Baptism"; "Catholics Enter 12-College Education Venture with Protestants"; "Catholic University Hires Southern Baptist to Teach Theology."

The Reverend David Bowman, S.J., has joined the staff of the National Council of Churches. Rev. James L. Empereur, S.J., from Decatur, Illinois, writes an article for a Catholic journal glowingly paying tribute to a new Lutheran breviary which he uses.

In Italy a Presbyterian is given permission to take communion and share fully in a mass at her wedding to a Catholic.

In Kansas City, Protestants and Catholics are getting together to establish a unified parish in the inner city.

In Schenectady, New York, Catholics and Protestants have got together to establish a coffee house called "The Dialogue."

In Todelo, Ohio, on the first Sunday of each month a Lutheran minister and a Catholic priest join in presenting a religious program on a local television station.

Not of great significance for the ecumenical movement —but perhaps of significance for the subject of this book— is this small item in the bulletin of St. John's Methodist Church in Edwardsville, Illinois: "The St. Boniface CYO wishes to invite the members of the St. John's Methodist Church high school youth group to a dance to be held Sunday from 8–11 p.m. There will be a live band and we ask that you do not wear shorts or slacks."

In St. Louis, under the auspices of Webster College (Catholic), a six-grade elementary school has been started with religion taught jointly by a nun on the college faculty and a member of the staff of a nearby Protestant seminary.

A Catholic priest from Baxter Springs, Kansas—population 4,000—writes: "Our Catholic and Methodist people have just begun the 'Living Room Dialogues' . . . There is no theological problem with baseball and my best Mass servers have 'First Baptist' blazoned on their uniforms. I think it is time for us to unite in many areas of youth activity; is it possible for the CYO to become the Christian Youth Organization, perhaps? . . . Fellowship (the word Catholics for so long wouldn't use) is important in itself, but it has to be deeper than playing golf together. If it is, you have no idea where genuine concern will lead one. It becomes the charity that does not envy and cannot be provoked. Dr. Martin E. Marty expressed it once with his usual pungency. We happened to be flying over his former Lutheran parish just outside Chicago; he mentioned that after he had received some national honor, the neighboring Catholic pastor cited it at all the Masses and suggested, with exquisite courtesy, that the parishioners might each telephone, not Dr. Marty, but one of his Lutheran parishioners to offer congratulations. 'And,' Marty said, 'you know you just can't have religious war with that kind of thing going on.' "[8]

Probably not noted in any theological journal was a small item from the March 9, 1966 *Area News,* a weekly community newspaper at Gillespie, Illinois:

A Catholic priest sent his entire week's salary to help start a fund to rebuild the Baptist church, which was completely demolished by the tornado that hit Jackson, Miss., last week.

Father Gierut, of the Bunker Hill-Wilsonville parish, said the picture of the demolished Baptist Church on the front page of the *Alton Evening Telegraph* brought recollections of the "grief-stricken memories of the tornado which hit Bunker Hill seventeen years ago and destroyed our St. Mary's Catholic Church and parish rectory to level ground.

"It was impossible for our small group of parishioners to commence rebuilding the church, because their own homes, furniture and all belongings were lost in this catastrophe. It was through the aid of our Bishop and the hundreds of letters from Protestants, with contributions, which gave us the courage to tackle the burdensome project of rebuilding the church."

At the meeting of the members of the Altar Society the priest said: "Our parish has experienced the generous aid of others when we were in need. It is our turn to reciprocate and extend a helping hand to a church in this hour of tragedy."

He suggested [that members] in this season of Lent perform some act of personal sacrifice and give up some form of amusement, shows, dancing, parties, candy, cigarettes, and forward dollars of sacrifice to help rebuild Woodville Heights Baptist Church in Jackson, Miss.

That is not big news—but maybe it is.

All of these items—many of them frowned upon by the more conservative Catholic and Protestant leaders—are creating a new atmosphere. The number of such incidents certainly will grow.

THEOLOGY AND UNITY

The theological basis and need for greater unity is now widely recognized, even though actual unification is nowhere in sight.

Christ's prayer for unity for his followers—as well as St. Paul's choice of marriage as a symbol of the unity of the church with Christ—are now being taken more seriously than they have been for centuries, and have caused deep-seated changes in outlook.

Perhaps this is best symbolized in the publication of *The Documents of Vatican II,* with two introductions to the United States edition: one by Cardinal Shehan, archbishop of Baltimore, and the other by Protestant Bishop Reuben H. Miller, then president of the National Council of the Churches of Christ in the U.S.A.

The Decree on Ecumenism of the Second Vatican Council stated: "Catholics must joyfully acknowledge and esteem the truly Christian endowments from our common heritage which are to be found among our separated brethren. It is right and salutary to recognize the riches of Christ and virtuous works in the lives of others who are bearing witness to Christ."

Later the same document notes:

> The Christian way of life of these [separated] brethren is nourished by faith in Christ. It is strengthened by the grace of baptism and the hearing of God's Word. This way of life expresses itself in private prayer, in meditation on the Bible, in Christian family life, and in services of worship offered by Communities assembled to praise God. Furthermore, their worship sometimes displays notable features of an ancient, common liturgy.
>
> The faith by which they believe in Christ bears fruit in praise and thanksgiving for the benefits received from the hands of God. Joined to it are a lively sense of justice and a true neighborly charity. This active faith has produced many organizations for the relief of spiritual and bodily distress, the education of youth, the advancement of humane social conditions, and the promotion of peace throughout the world.
>
> And if in moral matters there are many Christians who do not always understand the gospel in the same way as Catholics, and do not admit the same solutions for the more difficult problems of modern society, nevertheless they share our desire to cling to Christ's word. . . .[9]

Increasingly all Christians view their faith not as an object to be used on Sunday morning—where divisions are more obvious—but something to be believed and a way of life to be lived. Faith is not to be carefully guarded and kept on an honored shelf, but must be applied to the dirt and grime and tragedy of life. In a very real sense all of life is a service of worship, and the few hours we are separated in a particular type of worship are small when compared with the other times and ways we worship together. As this type of thinking and working together becomes more and more common, understanding among Christians will grow.

And so—inevitably—will the number of Protestant-Catholic marriages.

When a survey of the Christian Reformed church in the United States showed about four times as many Christian Reformed-Catholic weddings as informal estimates had indicated, the denominational paper, *The Banner,* commented: "Cupid is no ardent student of theology, and a far more potent factor in the ecumenical movement than churchmen may suppose."[10]

NOTES TO CHAPTER I

1. John L. Thomas, S.J., *The American Catholic Family* (Englewood Cliffs, N.J.: Prentice-Hall, 1956), 2nd ed., p. 154.
2. Harvey J. Locke, "Interfaith Marriages," *Social Problems,* April 1955.
3. Lee G. Burchinal and Loren E. Chancellor, "Factors Related to Interreligious Marriages in Iowa, 1953–57," Research Bulletin 510, November 1962, issued by Iowa State University. These figures are found in Appendix A.
4. James H. S. Bossard and Eleanor Stoker Boll, *One Marriage, Two Faiths* (New York: Ronald Press, 1957), p. 59.
5. C. Stanley Lowell, *Protestant-Catholic Marriage* (Nashville, Tenn.: Broadman Press, 1962), p. 4.
6. Dominion (Canada) Bureau of Statistics.

7. *Commonweal,* May 13, 1960.
8. Rev. Joseph T. Nolan, "Ecumenism Comes to Baxter Springs," *National Catholic Reporter,* May 25, 1966.
9. This and all future quotations from the documents of Vatican II are taken from *The Documents of Vatican II,* Walter M. Abbott, S.J., ed. (New York: Guild Press, American Press, and Association Press, 1966).
10. Donald H. Bouma, "Religiously Mixed Marriages: Denomination Consequences in the Christian Reformed Church," *The Banner,* April 21, 1961, quoted in *Marriage and Family Living,* November 1963.

II

There Are Problems, But...

We have been married almost seven years as this is being written; we have two children; we have faced some problems and we will have to face more.

We are not suggesting in this book that the Protestant-Catholic marriage will not face problems.

Any marriage will face problems.

This book is an attempt to encourage those already married and those yet to be married to face these problems realistically, so that what appears to be an obstacle to a happy marriage may become a stepping-stone to a happier marriage.

If you are reading this and you and your spouse-to-be are both eighteen, *don't* get married—not because one is Protestant and one Catholic, but because you may not be mature enough yet, and that immaturity probably includes your religious life.

If you and your future partner have known each other only three months, *don't* get married yet—not because of your different religious background but because you should get to know each other better.

There is a great variety of factors to be considered in approaching a marriage, *one* of which is religious affiliation and outlook. Marriage brings many problems which necessitate adjustments by each partner. Religious differences require added accommodations by each person and so should be considered seriously and as objectively as possible by a couple before marriage.

The matter of religious beliefs in relation to marriage has not been studied as thoroughly as it should be, as thoroughly as we hope it eventually will be. One article on the question noted correctly: "Many generalizations from various studies as to the degree and consequences of interreligious marriages are open to question."[1]

WHAT SURVEYS SHOW

Because of limited statistics within the United States, there has been relatively little good research of marriage risks and marriage conflicts because of a Protestant-Catholic marriage. Several of these surveys have suggested great dangers for such a marriage; others have indicated that this danger has been overestimated—but not surprisingly the studies which paint the gloomy pictures are the ones which Protestant and Catholic periodicals generally publish.

What are the studies and what do they show?

There is general agreement up to this point that a Protestant-Catholic marriage faces more risks than does one between Catholics or one between Presbyterians.

A 1938 survey of a number of Maryland youth found divorce and desertion occurring as shown in Table VII.[2]

A survey in the state of Washington published in 1943 had somewhat similar results, with Catholic parents scor-

Table VII

Percentage of Divorces and Desertions, Maryland Survey

Both parents Jewish...................................... 4.6
Both parents Catholic.................................. 6.4
Both parents Protestants............................. 6.8
Mixture of above.. 15.2
No church affiliation..................................... 16.7

ing best and those with no affiliation having a much higher rate of divorce than in the Maryland study.[3]

A survey in Michigan by the respected sociologist, Judson T. Landis, had results somewhat similar to the Washington study.[4]

While all of the above studies must be considered by any serious student, the two areas which would appear to provide the best opportunities for a thorough study are Canada and Iowa, where statistics are kept on the religious affiliation of those marrying. Unfortunately, Canada does not keep similar records on divorce.

But in Iowa Lee G. Burchinal and Loren E. Chancellor used the data available in that state to publish a little-noted, but most significant, study of 72,485 marriages.[5]

They broke down the Protestant religious affiliation into the various segments, and separated those being married both by age and economic status.

The over-all picture on survival rates (100 being the ideal) is shown in Table VIII.

One of the clear conclusions of this study is that the greatest risk is the person who simply defines himself as "a Protestant," with no particular affiliation. Probably most people who have no affiliation consider themselves in some vague way Protestants, and declare themselves as such on any form. The result is that they should perhaps be more properly categorized as "unchurched" or "no affiliation."

Table VIII

Percentage of Marriage Survivals, Iowa Survey

Both Catholic	96.2
Presbyterian-Protestant (other than Presbyterian)	94.6
Both Lutheran	94.1
Both Protestant (smaller groups)	94.0
Lutheran-Protestant	93.0
Methodist-Protestant	92.9
Both Methodists	91.4
Both Presbyterian	91.0
Catholic-Lutheran	90.5
Baptist-Protestant	90.5
Catholic-Presbyterian	89.8
Both Baptist	89.8
Catholic-Protestant (smaller groups)	89.1
AVERAGE FOR TOTAL POPULATION	87.6
Catholic-Methodist	83.8
Unspecified Protestant-Protestant	82.7
Catholic-Baptist	81.6
Both unspecified Protestant	35.0
Catholic-Unspecified Protestant	28.7

Their presence in previous studies brings down the Catholic-Protestant marriage survival rate considerably.

The authors of the Iowa study noted: "One of the important findings of the present investigation is that the lower survival rates of interreligious marriages were derived mainly from the marriages of Catholics with persons who apparently were not affiliated with any Protestant denomination. Apparently the clash of religious values and beliefs less frequently led to divorce in the interreligious marriages than did circumstances associated with the lack of affiliation or identification with a church by the non-Catholic partner."

In pointing this out we do not suggest that the religious differences which do exist are unimportant to the couple involved, where both maintain a loyalty to their original

religious moorings. These differences are real and sometimes must be compromised in realistic situations. This
may not be easy. But the Iowa study suggests that these
compromises are less painful than adjustments which must
be made between a couple when one has only a nominal
affiliation.

Other studies by the same Iowa authors pinpoint the
youthful marriage as the one having the greatest hazards.
The rate of youthful marriages among those who classify
themselves as religiously unaffiliated, or who specify no
affiliation, is markedly higher than those specifying either
Catholic or some branch of Protestantism.[6]

Among other things the Iowa study shows that with the
exceptions of the Catholic-Methodist, Catholic-Baptist, and
Catholic-Unspecified Protestant marriages, Catholics marrying Protestants have a better than average chance of
having their marriage survive.

It is still true, according to this survey, that two Catholics marrying, or two Presbyterians marrying, or two Lutherans marrying have a slightly better chance of marital
success. But the differences are very small. Only slightly
more than one percentage point separates a Catholic-Presbyterian marriage from a Presbyterian-Presbyterian marriage, for example.

Within two percentage points of each other are the following: both Methodist, both Presbyterian, Catholic-Lutheran, Baptist-Protestant, Catholic-Presbyterian, and both
Baptist.

The same study shows that statistically the ages of those
being married and their economic status may have more to
do with the chances of survival of the marriage than the
religious affiliation; the younger the persons being married
the greater the hazard, and the lower the economic status,

the more the danger of marital collapse exists. The Washington study cited earlier in this chapter found that a Protestant-Catholic marriage in the economic class of "professional" had a 5.56 per cent divorce rate, while the divorce rate for two Catholics in the category of "semi-skilled" was 10.61 per cent—almost twice as high.

In a general way it can then be said of Catholic-Protestant marriages that they increased somewhat the danger of divorce, but the Iowa study also indicates that the sweeping generalizations made in the past are not valid.

DESERTION AND UNHAPPINESS

Divorce is not the only danger a marriage faces. Two other dangers are desertion and unhappiness.

A study of desertion published in 1954 comes to the conclusion: "Mixed marriages may (or may not) be more prone to end in divorce, but they show no undue tendency toward desertion."[7]

A valuable but unpublished doctoral thesis by Richard N. Hey made a research project of marital conflict in interreligious marriages compared with those where both partners have the same affiliation. This covered not only Protestants and Catholics, but also Jews. His study came to the conclusion that in the area of marital conflict, virtually no difference exists between the interfaith and same-faith marriages.[8] A study which differs slightly came to the conclusion that in the Catholic wife-Protestant husband situation there was no significant difference in happiness when compared to the unmixed marriage, but in the case of the Protestant wife-Catholic husband it found a tendency to less happiness in such a marriage.[9] Other studies have found much the same. Part of the difficulty here appears to be related to the situation where the Protestant wife is attempting—or not attempting—to bring up the children in the Catholic church.

It could be added that all studies made to this point may become relatively obsolete in view of the changing attitudes of the churches. The goodwill among churches (which after all are people) eventually is bound to be reflected in the changing of public attitudes.

Perhaps more typical than most church authorities would like to admit is this experience of a Catholic wife of an Episcopalian:

> Our marriage has been stimulated and enriched by the challenge of walking separate paths to God, but ever hand in hand. . . . Considering the assets of a mixed marriage, we believe of prime importance the fact that such a union can foster and encourage a more Christian, harmonious and charitable relationship in every aspect of marriage. When we acknowledge and concede that two individuals, though they be married, do not necessarily think alike, we are more apt to respect differences of opinion. . . . There is nothing in the marriage ceremony that requires one partner to become a carbon copy of the other. . . . When our boys [growing up as Catholics] marry, I would much prefer they chose devout, convinced Methodists, Presbyterians or members of other faiths, than nominal Catholics. With a wife whose faith is a guiding force in her life, not just a shell to don on Sunday, I believe quite firmly they can build a good and lasting marriage. If these opinions, thoughts and conclusions seem too optimistic, if it appears I'm looking through rose-colored glasses, it is only because they are derived from our personal experience.[10]

This does not mean that all difficulties for your marriage —or your proposed marriage—are in the past. The various studies show that the Protestant-Catholic marriage should

be approached with caution, with eyes wide open.
But not with despair.

NOTES TO CHAPTER II

1. Loren E. Chancellor and Thomas P. Monahan, "Religious Preferences and Interreligious Mixtures in Marriages and Divorces in Iowa," *American Journal of Sociology,* November 1955.
2. Howard M. Bell, *Youth Tell Their Story* (Washington, D. C.: American Council on Education, 1938), p. 21.
3. H. Ashley Weeks, "Differential Divorce Rate by Occupation," *Social Forces,* March 1943.
4. Judson T. Landis, "Marriages of Mixed and Non-Mixed Religious Faiths," *American Sociological Review,* June 1949.
5. Lee G. Burchinal and Loren E. Chancellor, "Survival Rates Among Religiously Homogamous and Interreligious Marriages," *Social Forces,* May 1963.
6. Loren E. Chancellor and Lee G. Burchinal, "Status Levels of Grooms, Religious Affiliations and Ages of Brides and Grooms, Iowa, 1953–57," Journal Paper Project No. 1447, Iowa State University. See Table 1.
7. Thomas P. Monahan and William M. Kephart, "Divorce and Desertion by Religious and Mixed-Religious Groups," *American Journal of Sociology,* March 1954.
8. Richard N. Hey, "Dissimilarity of Religious Background of Marital Partners as a Factor in Marital Conflict," unpublished doctoral thesis, Columbia University, 1963, pp. 76–98.
9. Rev. Vincent dePaul Mathews, "A Study on the Nature and Frequency of Marital Problems and Their Relationship to Certain Sociological Factors in Catholic Marriages," unpublished doctoral thesis, St. Louis University, 1962, pp. 98–100.
10. Mrs. Mary Gregory Low in *Mixed Marriages* (St. Meinrad, Ind.: Abbey Press, 1966), pp. 92–107.

III

The Wrong Solution: Indifference

Perhaps the greatest danger facing the couple in a Protestant-Catholic marriage is religious indifference. Unfortunately, by their attitudes, many churches simply encourage this indifference; the person who has dared to violate the written or unwritten rules by marrying a fellow Christian of another affiliation is too often made to feel like an outsider. "I went to church a few Sundays after I married Trudy but the people at church treated me as if I had leprosy," one man who married a Catholic girl told us. He feels he cannot in good conscience join her church, so now he attends none. If he had married a weak fellow-Presbyterian, everyone would have congratulated him, but marrying a good Catholic was terrible.

As a 1966 document from the World Council of Churches correctly noted: "In the past, the churches have primarily warned against mixed marriages. . . . But warning is not the real pastoral task of the churches. They must rather recognize and accept mixed marriages, instead of regarding them as an anomaly, a mistake to be corrected.

The attitude which seeks only to prevent, and denies further responsibility, necessarily leads to estrangement from the Church."[1]

The individual couple cannot do much to change church attitudes, but they can take a look at themselves and their future.

Statistical studies are almost nonexistent in this field, and what studies there are have limited value. They do indicate that indifference too often is the result for one or both parties in a Protestant-Catholic marriage, although in fairness it must be stated that often there may not have been much interest prior to such a marriage. Confirming this trend toward indifference is the Iowa study which showed that for a five-year period, in the case of the Catholic groom-Protestant bride marriages, 17.2 per cent were civil rather than religious ceremonies, and in the case of the Protestant groom-Catholic bride marriages, 32.4 per cent were civil rather than religious ceremonies. Both figures are substantially above the 4.5 per cent for two Protestants and 7.9 per cent for two Catholics.[2] While the fact that a marriage took place under civil rather than religious auspices does not necessarily mean that either or both partners are religiously indifferent, we tend to believe that a study in depth might develop at least some relationship between the two—and that a marriage ordinarily should begin under religious auspices if there is to be a sense of Christian direction in the home.

In a study of 743 "mixed" marriages in a community which could in no sense be considered typical, the following conclusion was reached: "Of 444 men who were involved in a Roman Catholic-Protestant marriage, 110 no longer had even a nominal connection with their old church, and 124 had not attended church in the preceding year. Of the 449 wives involved in such marriages, 60 claimed no church affiliation and 91 had not attended church in the preceding year. . . . Only 22 of the 206 husbands who were reared in the Roman Catholic church attended as frequently as every other Sunday."[3] The limitation of this study is not only the community studied, but also the fact that no comparison was made of the figures cited above with a similar sampling of marriages where both were from the same church. The author of the study strongly implies—probably correctly—that indifference is too frequently the result in the Protestant-Catholic marriage.

One book—published as late as 1962—suggests that "the only possibility of survival" of a Protestant-Catholic marriage is "that one of the partners might become completely indifferent to his own faith."[4]

The evidence completely fails to support such a conclusion.

The Iowa study referred to in the previous chapter shows clearly that the greatest risk in the Protestant-Catholic marriage is the "unspecified Protestant," who in reality is nothing, who is indifferent. All studies show that the greatest risks are those with no church affiliation, and indifference is almost the same thing, though a nominal affiliation may continue.

So even from the desire to see a marriage succeed—forgetting all religious considerations entirely—it makes sense for a person to remain an active church member.

AREAS OF AGREEMENT

It should be kept in mind that what Christians of differing affiliations share is much greater than any areas of disagreement, though the stress of some on areas of disagreement rather than agreement has distorted the viewpoint of many. Your marriage—or proposed marriage—is a good reason to take inventory of yourself, and part of that inventory must be an awareness of what you and other Christians share, as well as areas of difference.

You probably accept the same basic creeds: The Apostles' and the Nicene. You recite the same Lord's Prayer, and on most subjects your Protestant church and your Catholic church are in accord. Many Protestant and Catholic theologians now are in agreement on the most divisive doctrinal issue of the Reformation: justification. Most important of all, you are united with the same Saviour, and this unity in Christ should be recognized as potentially the dominant factor in your life together.

And as one author notes: "To be thankful for the heritage of faith that could produce such a lovable person [as your partner] is a constant source of strength and renewal. One can never feel completely alien before the altar that helped produce the person one loves."[5]

Some people with emotional problems feel that they must look down on someone because his skin is a different color, or his beliefs are different; if that description fits you, you had better either not enter this marriage (or perhaps any) or you had better face up to some of the realities about yourself. These attitudes may indicate an emotional immaturity on your part which will maximize differences between your partner and yourself.

The brother of one of the authors is a Lutheran minister in New York City. He and several other Lutheran ministers meet regularly with some Catholic priests to discuss doctrinal matters and social problems. All find themselves more in agreement with each other in both fields than with many others who happen to share their respective church affiliations.

While most writers express concern about religious indifference in a Protestant-Catholic marriage, and the authors' observations also indicate this can be the result, an Episcopal bishop has noted: "An initial diversity of religious faith, which may at the outset present more difficulty than a more homogenous situation, has at least the advantage of bringing the matter of religion in the marriage to the fore, with the result that if a solution is found the marriage is usually better grounded religiously than where the couple has not been forced to take so seriously the spiritual aspect of their union."[6]

We suggest one of two courses for anyone entering—or in—a Protestant-Catholic marriage.

1. Become active within your own church.
2. If you have never been active, and rarely attended church in the past, consider affiliating with your spouse's church.

The second suggestion may be misunderstood. You should not join a church because your John or Jane wants you to. It should be approached slowly, carefully, and because you genuinely believe you can in good conscience.

A Catholic study shows that an unusually high percentage of cases where a "conversion" has taken place ends up in Catholic chancery court. Father Thomas observes: "The percentage of converts at marriage [appearing in chancery courts] is of interest because it is believed that many of these conversions at marriage may have been occasioned more out of a desire to please the Catholic

party than through conviction."[7] Changes of affiliation to
a Protestant church have the same dangers.

In the community study mentioned earlier in this chapter, 39 Roman Catholics joined the Protestant church of
their husband or wife, and 33 Protestants joined the Roman Catholic church. Of the total of 72 who "converted,"
only 23 "attended the spouse's church as frequently as
every other Sunday. The change in many instances was
frankly made in order to secure peace in the family, generally for the sake of the children."[8]

One writer in the field offers this good advice: "Never
employ methods of coercion by which you try to force your
spouse to become a member of your denomination group,
and make equally sure that no undue and coercive pressure is brought to bear by your parents or other relatives.
Such ill-advised attempts to force a spouse to leave his
church and join one's own have only too often proved ill-
fated and blasted marital happiness. Even if your spouse
should be ready to join your church merely to keep peace,
you would have gained nothing. He would always have an
undercurrent of resentment in his heart, and his interest in
the church would be anything but genuine. The use of
force is never more out of place and productive of less
good than in the sphere of religion. . . . I know of no case
in which nagging contributed anything but a negative result."[9]

The Hey Study on marital conflict in what he calls "inter-faith" marriages has this significant statement: "The
one analysis in this investigation which did reveal a significant difference in the amount and intensity of marital
conflict was the comparison of those inter-faith couples in
which one partner had converted to the faith of the spouse,

with those inter-faith couples in which each spouse maintained his own religious affiliation. Conversion is positively related to marital conflict. . . . Whether the conversions reported in this investigation were voluntary or not is not known. Spouses who marry across religious lines and maintain their previous religious identity are able to cope with such differences with less conflict than spouses, one of whom changes religious identity. This finding is related to guilt on the part of the convert for abandoning parental values, and on the part of the 'winner' for getting his or her own way. Resentment for having to be the one to 'give in' also helps produce greater conflict, and the person who has maintained his faith may view the partner as weaker than himself, more easily dominated, and therefore less to be respected."[10]

The above statement is a sweeping generalization about the findings of one study, and obviously does not apply in many cases. But it also indicates that change in affiliation ("conversion" is ordinarily not the right word) should not be made without great care and understanding. Under no circumstances should force or pressure be used. It should not be done to please the relatives. If a change is made by either partner, it should not be with the attitude that one affiliation is superior to another, particularly on the part of the spouse whose affiliation has been changed. Exactly the wrong attitude is expressed in some of the books in this field, written, of course, from a particular Protestant or Catholic slant. One, for example, states: "Any Protestant considers his own faith, or that of any other Protestant, superior to Roman Catholicism."[11] Few Protestants would hold that—and if they do, they should hang their heads in shame. There are also unfortunately a few Roman Catholics who have the same heady ideas in reverse.

AVOIDING RELIGIOUS INDIFFERENCE

In his Encyclical on Christian Marriage, Pope Pius XI speaks about marriages between Catholics and Protestants bringing about "a headlong descent into religious indifference."

There is evidence that too frequently that has been the case. This can be avoided by four simple rules:

1. *Each partner must resolve to be active within his church.*

2. *At no time and under no circumstances should either partner speak with disrespect of the beliefs of the other.* Frequently Catholic priests and Protestant ministers suggest a brief informational course on the beliefs of their particular church, before a marriage takes place. Ideally, both the Protestant and Catholic partners should attend these classes together, and while each learns something about his spouse's religion—and frequently something about his own —both also should acquire some basic respect for the beliefs of the prospective partner. Marriage partners who remain relatively ignorant of the beliefs of the other almost inevitably take a "mine is superior" attitude. It is easy from that point to descend to the next level of blaming something you dislike in your partner's conduct on religious background. The best way to avoid this pitfall is to become reasonably well informed about your partner's religious heritage.

A balanced sense of humor is always a helpful thing in a marriage, and this should include religious affairs—but the humor must never be derisive. Unfortunately too much religious "humor" falls into that category.

3. *Each partner should go out of his way to encourage*

the other in church activities. This means more than going to church on Sunday morning. It means encouraging active participation in men's and women's groups, attending special masses or teaching a Sunday-school class, or whatever the activities may be in your particular churches.

4. *Each partner should encourage the other to help in those missions of the church which they can do together: living concern for your fellow human being.* That may get the two of you involved in something as unglamorous as getting a sewer system for a community; it may cause you to move to a poorer section of your city; it may involve you in teaching unlettered people to read and write. Literally hundreds of opportunities exist for you no matter where you live.

Those four rules are not difficult, and if they are followed, the major pitfall in a Protestant-Catholic marriage is avoided.

NOTES TO CHAPTER III

1. "Marriage and the Division Among the Churches," June 1966, a joint statement by the WCC Secretariat for Faith and Order and the WCC Department on the Cooperation of Men and Women in Church, Family, and Society.
2. Lee G. Burchinal and Loren E. Chancellor, "Factors Related to Interreligious Marriages in Iowa, 1953–57," Research Bulletin 510, November 1962, issued by Iowa State University.
3. Murray H. Leiffer, "Mixed Marriages and Church Loyalties," *Christian Century,* January 19, 1949.
4. C. Stanley Lowell, *Protestant-Catholic Marriages* (Nashville, Tenn.: Broadman Press, 1962), p. 78.
5. William H. Genné, "Building a Home on Two Altars," *Christian Home,* January 1966.
6. James A. Pike, *If You Marry Outside Your Faith* (New York: Harper and Brothers, 1954), pp. 10–11.
7. John L. Thomas, S.J., *The American Catholic Family* (Englewood Cliffs, N.J.: Prentice-Hall, 1956), 2nd ed., pp. 189–90.
8. Leiffer, *op. cit.*

9. O. A. Geiseman, *Make Yours a Happy Marriage* (St. Louis: Concordia, 1946), pp. 47–49.
10. Richard N. Hey, "Dissimilarity of Religious Background of Marital Partners as a Factor in Marital Conflict," unpublished doctoral thesis, Columbia University, 1963, pp. 107–8.
11. Lowell, *op. cit.*, p. 25.

IV

Learn What You Share and Share What You Can

The Protestant-Catholic marriage is in reality an *intra*faith marriage, not an *inter*faith marriage.

Unity is a gift of Christ to his followers, and in that unity you share. St. Paul writes: "There is neither Jew nor Greek, there is neither slave nor free, there is neither male nor female; for you are all one in Christ Jesus." (Galatians 3:28) This is a living reality for your marriage—and not something which any church has the option to give or take away. In Ephesians the same author speaks of Christ breaking down "the dividing wall of hostility," a wall which many still try to erect and preserve, and ironically, in the name of Christ. Even one of the most conservative of Protestant bodies, the Lutheran Church, Missouri Synod, at a recent convention noted: "Every Christian . . . enters into a real and living unity with every other member of Christ's holy body." This same note was sounded again and again at the history-making meetings of Vatican Council II.

This means that what Christian churches hold in common is much greater than what separates them. It is perhaps more correct to talk about "Who" we share than "What" we share. Despite the host of differences in doctrine and practice, the presence of Christ in your home or in your church should be a great unifying factor. And this so dominates the Christian landscape—or should—that other matters seem insignificant by comparison. Yet these "other matters" are also important, and this is why it is well worth your time to learn as much as possible about the heritage which you share with your partner.

This study you should experience yourself. Both the Protestant and Catholic partners to a marriage ought to learn everything they can about their own beliefs and the beliefs of the other. As Vatican Council II noted: "We must come to understand the outlook of our separated brethren. Study is absolutely required for this, and should be pursued with fidelity to truth and in a spirit of good will."[1]

There are a number of practical methods of doing this.

DISCUSSION AND READING

One way which can be effective—and can also be a waste of time—is to get acquainted with a priest or minister and chat informally. Perhaps you can take him out to lunch, or arrange to have a cup of coffee with him. This should be in addition to any other informational instructions the Protestant or Catholic party may be requested to take; the weakness of such instruction is that it tends to be somewhat stilted, it is frequently assumed you are not interested but simply forced to listen for a short period, and the information given is often the kind of basic information any halfway alert Protestant or Catholic already knows anyway. The informal chat with a pastor or priest is something beyond the formal instruction each partner may feel obligated to take; the minister or priest ordinarily will welcome such an opportunity.

Both parties to a Protestant-Catholic marriage should learn that among other things which you share are clergy who are human beings, who sometimes do not put the finest foot forward for your particular church. This does not mean they are not sincere, but sometimes either ability or tact may be lacking a little. If that happens in your case, don't blame your partner's church; if you look around you can find similar examples in your own. It may very well also be that the priest or minister who is not helpful in an informal visit is excellent at bringing comfort to the afflicted and dying, or has other gifts.

Because you may meet a clergyman with limited abilities in this particular area does not really limit your opportunity to learn.

There is a variety of good books available.

If you are a Protestant wanting to learn about the Catholic church, reading one or two of the several excellent books by Father Hans Kueng would be helpful, or perhaps *The Spirit of Catholicism* by Father Karl Adams, good though a little outdated. *The Riddle of Roman Catholicism,* by Dr. Jaroslav Pelikan, is a distinguished Protestant theologian's look at the Catholic church, also a little outdated, but well done. *Living Room Dialogues* may be helpful, a paperback in popular language.

Similar books about Protestantism are difficult to recommend because of the great diversity within Protestantism. The particular branch in which your marriage is involved undoubtedly has something worth reading. Of general application would be Robert McAfee Brown's *The Spirit of Protestantism.*

Good background would be Dr. Martin E. Marty's *History of the Christian Church.* Also excellent is Roland Bainton's *Horizon History of Christianity.* Both books are available in paperback.

The best book with background on church views of Protestant-Catholic marriages is *Mixed Marriage,* a 75-cent paperback published by the Abbey Press of St. Meinrad, Indiana. It is primarily a theological discussion of the issue, not designed specifically for the couple involved, but nevertheless good background for any couple or counselor.

Probably as important as any books you read are magazines and newspapers. Here you can learn what is happening today, and sense the mood of a church in transition, or a church trying under difficult circumstances to live Christian love in an increasingly complex society. The Catholic publications might include:

> The diocesan publication where you live
> *National Catholic Reporter*
> *America*
> *Commonweal*

Protestant publications are more diverse, but they might include:

Christian Century
The "official organ" of the Protestant partner's church
A more independent journal within the same church

If you start talking about and reading about your church and your partner's church, you will not only have a better understanding of yourself and your partner, you will also discover that "theology" and "church doctrine"—which used to bring a yawn from you—are anything but dull. If you read the right things you should also begin to grow in comprehension of what life is really all about, and how you fit into "the big picture."

As you personally grow in knowledge, you and your marriage partner will find more and more basis for discussion of issues facing the church and society. There is a commonly held view: "There are two things you should never discuss: politics and religion." People who say this believe that every discussion must end in an argument, and arguing religion or politics is not profitable for anyone. But the house which establishes a taboo on discussing politics and religion is shallow. Your home should be a place where the day-to-day needs of man and the ultimate realities of God and man come together for frequent informal conversation.

Worship

Reading and talking are not enough.

You should worship together occasionally. (One couple to whom we showed the rough draft of this manuscript disagrees with our use of the word "occasionally" here. They write: "We think you should worship together *as often as possible,* especially in the courtship period when you're trying to learn of the other's beliefs, and when it is a little more practical than it is after the children arrive. You can't share communion but you can share other things, and if you worship together only 'occasionally' you don't give each other a chance to have real understanding.")

The late Msgr. J. D. Conway, Judge of the Marriage Court, Diocese of Davenport, Iowa, had a "Question Box" column in the *National Catholic Reporter* and *Our Sunday Visitor*. His column carried the following question and answer:

Question: My husband is not a Catholic. He did go to church with me for some time when we were first married. Then one Christmas he asked me to go to church with him. I told him I was not allowed to participate in the services at his church. Since that day he has not attended Mass with me.

Now that the church is in the "Ecumenical Age," he has been reading the different articles in the paper about it. I have a feeling that he may want to test "it" or "me."

If he asks, may I attend, for instance at Christmas or some special occasion? If so, how far do I go? Sing with them? Join in prayer?

I know I could never change my religion; it is part of me. It is me. I hope and pray some day it will be part of him. But what do I do now?

I knew when I married that we would have problems to face, but this ecumenical movement seems to be giving me new problems.

Answer: It may also offer new solutions for old problems. Can you blame your husband for ceasing to go to Mass with you? He was accommodating himself to your wishes every Sunday, and you could not grant a similar wish of his even on Christmas?

Certainly we must carefully avoid religious indifferentism; so there must be prudent limits as to how often you should accompany your husband to his church. But on the other hand marriage is said to be an arrangement of give and take on a 50–50 basis. Satisfactory results will seldom be attained when the division is 100 to 0. Without violating your own conscience you must show respect and consideration for your husband's religious convictions and traditions.

When you do go to his church for special occasions you are not constrained to sit there like old stone face exuding an aura of righteous disdain. There should be some good Christian hymns and prayers in which you can join. You can stand or sit when the others do. If they read the Gospel you should show some respect for the Lord's word. If they recite the Apostle's Creed you will probably find it identical with the one you know.

You as a Catholic do not attend the Protestant church for purposes of your own personal worship, but when you are there you need not disdain the honest Christian worship which is being offered by those around you.[2]

The only portion of that answer with which we disagree is the suggestion—which is at least implied—that the Catholic cannot sincerely worship in the Protestant church or the Protestant worship in the Catholic church. There may not be the comfortable feeling of worship as you have traditionally known it, but this does not mean you cannot worship.

We suggest that *at least* twice a year the Catholic partner should attend a Protestant service and *at least* twice a year the Protestant partner should attend a Catholic service. The result can only be greater understanding.

Particularly with the recent changes in Catholic liturgy, Protestants and Catholics may find a surprising similarity in the worship service of the other, though differences will continue to be apparent. Both who attend sincerely wanting to learn can find something to learn from the other; Catholics may find Protestant hymn-singing rather robust compared to that in their own congregation, where they are not accustomed to much hymn-singing; and Protestants may find the quiet and solemnity which precedes the mass a welcome and refreshing change from the clamor which is common in too many Protestant churches.

"I don't like going to Mass any more," an elderly Polish lady told us recently. "It's too much like going to a Protestant church service; I didn't grow up that way."

For her the changes are understandably unwelcome. But

for many the new Catholic liturgy will help bridge the gap between these two branches of Christendom. This is important when you realize that for most people the differences between churches are not viewed in terms of church doctrine, but church practice. By accommodating your church practices to each other a little without sacrificing a worshipful experience, you immeasurably speed reconciliation on issues more basic to theologians.

One practical approach to the problem of when to worship together is to do it when you are on vacation. (If you have no plans for a regular vacation, you should make them; you owe that to yourselves.) The two of us find it a little more natural and easy to attend Catholic and Lutheran services on a Sunday morning away from where we live than right here at home—although we probably should do it at home more than we do.

Keep in mind one other point: let each see your particular church at its best. Your local parish may not be the finest place to begin to understand your worship practices. If the organ squeaks or the choir is miserable or the pastor or priest preaches unbelievably dull sermons, don't be surprised if your partner is not too impressed by your service. There are probably some splendid sanctuaries of your church not too many miles away which may not be typical, but where the visitor gains more understanding and a better impression. Let your partner worship with you at your home church too, of course.

COMMON ACTION

Your Christian faith demands of you that your expressed beliefs be followed by concrete deeds; and in most of these concrete deeds the Protestant and Catholic can find a joint opportunity to live their faith, to make of their lives a common worship.

It will vary from the most undramatic and household type of chore to significant application of Christian love to the problems of society.

When Paul's (Lutheran) church has a fund-raising sausage supper, Jeanne usually bakes a pie for them to help out. When the ladies of Jeanne's (Catholic) church have a mother-daughter banquet, Paul helps the men in the kitchen.

There are a host of things we can attend together: church banquets, church and school dedications, an anniversary dinner for a priest or a minister, a concert by the Notre Dame University Glee Club or the Concordia Seminary Chorus, funerals and weddings, public lectures—the list could go on and on.

Jeanne speaks to the Lutheran PTA and Paul speaks to the Daughters of Isabella and the Knights of Columbus; we find no lack of a warm welcome, and if on occasion we stumble into an error caused by lack of familiarity with another church, we find people very forgiving and willing to smile at our foibles if we are willing to laugh at ourselves.

Both of us share an interest in a nearby Methodist school, McKendree College, and Paul's presence on the board of trustees or Jeanne's presence at a public lecture at this Methodist school does not divide us, but brings us closer together.

Paul serves on the advisory board of St. Joseph's Hospital in Highland, Illinois. Jeanne has been there for hospitalization. The sisters have gone out of their way to be helpful and kind, and we hope that in a small way we have reciprocated.

Both of us are interested in race relations. This we believe is a practical place where society needs the active concern of everyone who has the courage to call himself a Christian. This particular concern has led Paul to try to help establish an Urban League in our area, where we again find ourselves working closely with leaders of the Catholic and Protestant churches. This interest takes us to meetings of the Lutheran Human Relations Association and the Catholic Interracial Council, where both of us find our concerns are identical.

In many other areas we try—often most inadequately—to apply our beliefs to life around us: in our concerns for the mentally ill and retarded, in our concern over anti-Semitism among too many Christians, in our desire to see that government becomes more responsive to the needs of the poor and oppressed both at home and abroad.

If Christianity is viewed only as a matter of going to church on Sunday morning, then a Protestant-Catholic marriage might very well be divisive. But if Christianity is much more than that—as it must be—then we can celebrate our faith together in a hundred different ways each day, enriched by the added dimensions our differing backgrounds bring to our situation.

A widely used marriage guide states: "Those who are willing to make real sacrifices for ideal ends are certainly interested in something beyond themselves. And such concern for others is among the most important character essentials for success in marriage."[3]

In summary, then, we suggest that you:

1. Read and study together.
2. Worship together occasionally.

3. Work together in the many areas where your common faith demands your efforts.
4. Remember that you share a unity in Christ.

NOTES TO CHAPTER IV

1. Section 9 of Chapter II of the Decree of Ecumenism, *The Documents of Vatican II* (New York: Guild Press, America Press, Association Press, 1966), p. 353.
2. Msgr. J. D. Conway, "Question Box," *National Catholic Reporter,* April 6, 1966.
3. Sylvanus M. Duvall, *Before You Marry* (New York: Association Press, 1959), p. 23.

V

Don't Be Hard on Your Relatives

Much of marriage is a matter of adjustment.

Part of this adjustment in a Protestant-Catholic marriage is made by and with relatives who may be shocked to learn their son or their daughter is marrying a Catholic or Protestant. For generations they have been told: "Don't marry a Catholic," or "Don't marry a Protestant." The emotional scars of centuries of lovelessness between Protestants and Catholics may be found in your families—and your response to an occasional inappropriate remark should be quiet understanding and sympathy, when hostility and a sharp exchange might be more natural for your disposition.

Remember that many Catholics, who tend to associate mostly with Catholics, view the Protestant as the Puritan or early American who crudely denied all basic liberties to Catholics, or perhaps the tradition and emotion reaches back to a European country where Protestants waged war and persecuted Catholics; remember that for many Protestants, who travel socially largely among fellow-Protestants, the Catholic belongs to a church which is symbolized by the Inquisition, and Protestants tend to recall wars where Catholics were the aggressors. Both groups too often have a tendency to generalize about the other side on the basis of the abuses which both sides have committed over the years, but which are certainly not typical of either branch of Christendom today. But these "facts" have been drilled into people since childhood, and have resulted in certain emotional patterns which will change slowly *if* you show understanding.

Paul served part of his Army time in Germany and when he learned that a 20-year-old German with whom he had become acquainted was a Lutheran, Paul mentioned that he was also a Lutheran and was attending the local Lutheran church. "We haven't had anyone in our family marry a Catholic in more than 200 years," was the German's proud response. When Paul suggested they might attend church together the next Sunday, his German friend admitted that he had not been to church in about seven years, since the day he was confirmed. For this man and his family religion had become something you were against, rather than something you were for. Yet they had a strong family tradition and if he had married a Catholic girl his family would have been outraged, even though he was for all practical purposes not affiliated with any religious group, though he called himself a Lutheran.

This is an extreme example, but there can be no question that many families feel strongly on this issue.

OPPORTUNITIES FOR UNDERSTANDING

The Protestant-Catholic marriage may present some barriers to relatives, but it also presents some opportunities for the couple to quietly, gradually, lovingly get people to know and understand a differing Christian heritage—and this is no small contribution.

The authors have been fortunate that both of our families have overcome an initial reluctance and have shown an understanding and helpfulness that has meant much to us. Our visits with others who have entered a Protestant-Catholic marriage indicate that in most instances relatives do not make life difficult for the couple entering such an intrafaith marriage.

There have been some cases of extreme bad judgment on the part of relatives—and also by newly married couples—that have resulted in awkward situations. Perhaps the most extreme case of which we know is where a girl married a Catholic boy against her parents' wishes and they no longer speak to her. In this instance the parents of the girl needed Christian counseling more than their daughter. Such cases are few. Perhaps part of the difficulties some parents face when their son or daughter marries "an outsider" is that they feel they must have done something wrong. Those who marry Catholics or Protestants have been considered a little less loyal, a little less religious. The myth—and studies show this is exactly what it is—says that those who marry outside their family's religious moorings come from homes where there have been divorce, unhappiness, family fights, and lack of affection. All of these things they had heard and never questioned, and suddenly they face the situation with their own son or daughter. It should not surprise the prospective bride and groom if people who had heard this all their lives are deeply hurt, and that this feeilng will sometimes result in a period of tension with in-laws for the newly married.

In fairness it must be added that often when both the bride and groom are Baptists or both Catholics, friction develops with in-laws. To blame religion for the friction that sometimes develops with parents and relatives in a Protestant-Catholic marriage is frequently an inaccurate generalization. Religion may be blamed for the strife, but if this handy peg were not available, tensions would be blamed on something else—rarely the real cause.

One study of conflicts with parents, comparing "mixed marriages" with "same-faith" marriages—using the terminology of the study—came to the conclusion: "Contrary to popular expectations, disagreements about mothers and mothers-in-law are reported less often by [religiously] inter-married husbands. . . . Among wives it is again in the same-faith group that the greater amount of disagreement is mentioned."[1]

One study is not a sound basis for sweeping conclusions, but it is at least a good possibility that the frequently made assumption that Protestant-Catholic marriages result in unusual family difficulties is not valid.

There is, of course, the real possibility that the young couple anticipating difficulties tend to move away from the two families more than the partners in a same-affiliation marriage, and the result is more difficulties with parents in the same-affiliation marriage—not because of religion, but because of proximity.

Another study finds slightly more trouble with in-laws in the Protestant-Catholic marriage than in the same-church marriage.[2]

This whole area needs more research than it has received up to this point.

A 1959 Gallup poll may have some bearing on this

question. When asked whether they would object to their
child's marrying someone of the other church, 23 per cent
of Roman Catholic parents indicated they would object
and 35 per cent of Protestant parents said they would object. Since this poll was conducted prior to the great new
movements toward understanding, it is probable that a
similar poll conducted today would find a smaller number
of parents objecting.

And objections before a marriage do not necessarily
mean difficulties afterward.

All of this means that the picture is not as bleak as
many have painted it. In order to head off difficulties, here
are a few simple rules to follow:

1. Don't argue with your parents or your in-laws about
religion. Arguments are never won; they only create tensions.

2. Elsewhere in this book we stress the need to avoid
any comments which might be considered disrespectful of
your spouse's religious affiliation. This is doubly important
when any relatives are around, for they may believe they
catch some disrespect when none is intended.

3. If you do face ignorance or intolerance from any of
the relatives, respond with understanding rather than
anger. They have grown up in a different generation with
different attitudes. You have shaken them in the most personal way possible, and the result may be a deeply felt
hurt. If you go out of your way to show kindness and
consideration, eventually things probably will improve.

We want to stress again, however, that in the large majority of cases relatives present no barrier because of religion to your having a wholesome married life.

NOTES TO CHAPTER V

1. Richard N. Hey, "Dissimilarity of Religious Background of Marital Partners as a Factor in Marital Conflict," unpublished doctoral thesis, Columbia University, 1963, p. 84.
2. Rev. Vincent dePaul Mathews, "A Study on the Nature and Frequency of Marital Problems and Their Relationship to Certain Sociological Factors in Catholic Marriages," unpublished doctoral thesis, St. Louis University, 1962, p. 93.

VI
Your Home

The home of the couple in a Protestant-Catholic marriage can present both special problems and unusual opportunities.

To a great extent the happiness of that home is made up of "little things" which in the long run make the big things. If the little things become irritants, the marriage can easily start heading in the wrong direction.

AREAS FOR COMPROMISE

Here are a few practical areas where compromise is relatively easy, but conscious efforts have to be made in the right direction:

1. *Reading Material*

It is worth repeating that your home should be a place where both religious camps have magazines and books prominently displayed. That means that on occasion there will be an article with which you will find yourself in strong disagreement—but that happens also with periodicals and books published within your particular church.

It should not be necessary to add that the reading material is not there just for display purposes.

To a great extent laymen in the church—any church—are not used for anything more exciting than ushering on Sunday morning, counting the church collection, playing the organ, and singing in the choir. These are all good things, but unless and until more laymen understand a little of their church's theology and history, and have some feeling for the direction in which the church must go, laymen will continue to be good for fund-raising purposes, and women's organizations for making quilts, but neither for too much additional.

The Protestant-Catholic home has added reasons for learning as much as possible about church history, traditions, and thinking. This will come largely from the printed word.

Here it should be noted that the Christian's concerns are much broader than the specific church organization with which he is affiliated. His interest is humanity, and the newspapers, magazines, and books which are in the home should reflect this broad view. The "Christians" who in their home have only reading material with church sponsorship have really failed to understand some basic things about their faith.

2. *Pictures*

You can tell much about a home by the pictures which hang on the walls. A Protestant-Catholic home should agree on any picture before it goes up.

A Lutheran-Catholic home, for example, is not one where one partner insists that pictures of Martin Luther

hang in every room and the other wants pictures of Pope
Pius XII in every room.

The dashboard of your car need not be cluttered with
a small likeness of Mary for a Catholic wife and a Masonic
emblem for the husband.

All Christian churches have much good religious art in
common. This can attest to the unity in Christ which sym-
bolizes your home. This should not mean, however, if the
Methodist husband wants to hang a picture of John Wesley
in his study, that this is out of the question. The Catholic
wife may want a picture of Mary in the kitchen. Both
partners should show some flexibility and tolerance here.
A Protestant wife of a Catholic writes: "Both partners
should attempt to understand what is great about the persons the partner wants pictures of. The Protestant hopefully may come to want a Madonna around—Luther did!"
But if either party objects to a work of religious art, it
should not go up.

A crucifix, a Rembrandt showing Christ being taken
from the cross, or a modern painting depicting the love of
the Christian for people of all races and creeds and economic circumstances, can tell people something about your
home—and tell them in terms of unity and not conflict.

Religious art also presents an opportunity to say something additional. For example, in our home we display a
Jewish symbol made in Israel, which occasionally raises
questions. Since ours is a Lutheran-Catholic home, and a
country which was half-Lutheran and half-Catholic (Germany) committed unbelievable crimes against the Jews,
we want to make it clear that we feel a special sense of
kinship and obligation to the Jews. Recent studies show
that anti-Semitism is not dead among Christians, and we

want our home to do a little toward promoting under-standing.

Your circumstances may present your home with special opportunities to promote racial or religious understanding through art.

3. *Eating Habits*

This is not complicated. The Catholic partner does not eat meat on Friday during Lent and on certain other fast days. The simplest solution is for the Protestant partner to do the same. This makes cooking easier and creates no hardship on anyone.

We make an exception of that rule when we eat in res-taurants. Sometimes Paul joins Jeanne in eating a salad or a fruit plate or having shrimp or tuna. But if he feels like having a hamburger or roast beef, he does. Here there are no cooking problems. Even here, if the hamburger or roast beef presents too much temptation and difficulty for the Catholic partner, the Protestant should encourage the Catholic partner to live up to the obligations of his church by also avoiding meat even in the restaurant.

Avoiding meat on "fish days" when your Catholic chil-dren are present is also desirable.

The relaxation by the Catholic church of regulations about eating meat on Friday obviously has reduced dif-ficulties which might arise on this issue.

4. *Drinking Habits*

The Catholic-Lutheran or Catholic-Episcopal marriage (other Protestant examples could be cited) present few problems here, since the views of these churches on the drinking of alcoholic beverages is approximately the same: drunkenness is wrong, but drinking temperately is not.

The Catholic-Baptist home (and again other Protestant groups could be cited), however, may present some problems. Just as the Baptist should refrain from insisting on a steak on Friday during Lent, so the Catholic perhaps should be willing to forego his cocktail or glass of wine with a meal if it is offensive.

Nationally, excessive drinking is a leading cause of divorce and marital conflict, and obviously both partners in any type of marriage should avoid this.

5. *Money*

Something approaching a 50–50 arrangement on your contributions to your respective churches makes sense. Anything outside of this agreement should be mutually arrived at, and such things will arise. One church will have a building program and ask for pledges. Or perhaps both of you feel one church is carrying on a particularly worthy endeavor; or maybe one church is relatively impoverished; or the church which the children attend may alter your contribution pattern. This is something you should talk over. If you follow simple guidelines, which you can agree upon, there should be no major difficulty.

6. *Guests in Your Home*

One widely quoted book covering the subject of Protestant-Catholic marriages suggests that if, despite all the alarms sounded by the authors in the early chapters, the couple goes ahead and gets married anyway, then six possible "solutions" to avoid problems are suggested, one of them that the couple should live "in relative social isolation, that is, a withdrawal from most social contacts by the couple involved."[1]

That "solution" is like amputating your arm to cut your fingernails.

Obviously, there can be a problem if in your home only Catholics, or only Methodists, or only one religious group is welcome socially.

The easy and happy solution is to make sure that your home is open to all, and make sure that those who put their feet under your dining room table or kitchen table represent as wide a cross-section of the population as possible: economically, racially, and religiously.

We make it a point to welcome to our home Catholic and Lutheran clergymen—and many others as well. In the six years of our marriage our guests have included a Methodist bishop, an Episcopal priest, a Presbyterian minister, and other religious leaders; they have included a Protestant observer at the Vatican Council and Catholic priests ranging from a far-right conservative to a liberal monsignor. Guests in our home are Protestant, Catholic, and Jewish; they range from the resident of the worst slums in our area to the theology professor from India, from the John Birch Society leader to the man who calls himself a socialist. Our home is open to people of any race or nationality or creed or economic circumstance—and we believe we are richer for this experience.

The Protestant-Catholic couple should go out of their way to make sure that their friends and guests represent a diversity of viewpoints, both in religious affiliation and in other ways.

NOTES TO CHAPTER VI

1. James H. S. Bossard and Eleanor Stoker Boll, *One Marriage, Two Faiths* (New York: Ronald Press, 1957), p. 158.

VII
Your Children

Ideally the religious affiliation of the children should be decided before there is an engagement or marriage. If that is not done—or it is too late as you read this—then the decision should be made as quickly as possible, at the latest prior to the arrival of the children.

Children of a Protestant-Catholic marriage can grow up with unusual spiritual insights—or can grow up spiritually indifferent. The latter is a real danger in a Protestant-Catholic marriage, and is one which can be avoided if approached open-eyed and with understanding.

The worst advice is given by some prominent religious leaders: be fair, let the children decide. Dr. Norman Vincent Peale wrote: "I would maintain a scrupulously fair religious atmosphere in the home and, when the children are old enough, would let them decide their own religious faith for themselves. That is their right as sacred and sovereign personalities."[1] Another writer applauds a family which gave children at the age of twelve instruction in both the Catholic and Presbyterian beliefs, and then let the children choose.

While this approach has much appeal, the fact is that a child cannot and should not live in a religious vacuum until he is twelve years old, or twenty-one years old. The child should be attending church regularly long before he is twelve years old. If religion is not important in the life of a child before twelve, it is unlikely it ever will be important to him.

Another "solution" usually less than adequate is to bring the boys up in one church, the girls in another. A Lutheran pastor told us of this actual case: "I had a parishioner who had married a Roman Catholic lady. They had made the arrangement that the boys would go to his church, the girls to hers. They proceeded to have seven daughters and no sons! He came to me one day to ask whether (since all the babies had been born in a Roman Catholic hospital) I thought there had been some sort of 'hanky-panky,' whether pre- or post-natal. I assured him that I didn't think so. Obviously, this was not a good solution, at least not for this couple."

Recent statements by the Vatican and the World Council of Churches indicate that the trend may eventually be away from the requirement that children automatically must be brought up as Catholics if their parents were married by a Catholic priest; for the most part when this requirement is abolished it will result in positive good, and eliminate an unnecessary irritant which now exists between the churches. At the present time the Vatican and the World Council of Churches are engaged in dialogue on "Marriage in a Divided Church." High on the agenda is the matter of parental freedom in choosing the church affiliation for the children.

According to present official Catholic teaching, the Catholic partner has no choice in almost all cases, and must see that the children are baptized within the Catholic church and brought up as Catholics. For many this is a simple answer to a complex problem. The only exception is when permission is received through the bishop to waive this particular requirement.

KNOTTY PROBLEMS

Until the day comes when the present agreement is no longer required of Catholics, there will be some knotty problems. No one who makes such an agreement dare dismiss it lightly, but the present situation unfortunately forces people to sometimes choose the lesser of two evils.

Tom and Jane were married in the local Catholic church. Tom is a Catholic and Jane a Methodist. They were married by the priest to please Tom's parents; Tom actually didn't care much one way or another. Jane signed the pledge to bring up the children as Roman Catholics, doing it in good conscience and with every intent of fulfilling the words read to her. But Tom rarely attends mass, while Jane is at her Methodist church every Sunday and remains active. She finds it increasingly difficult to follow through on her original intent, so much so that she now has fears—not that her children will be Catholics, but that they may become poor Catholics.

Looking at it coldly from the statistical viewpoint, Jane should bring them up as Methodists—and Tom has no objections.

Most cases are not clear-cut, unfortunately, but when the couple is in agreement that to attempt to continue to follow the pledge might present real problems for the children, then difficult decisions may have to be made.

One thing must be said in favor of the agreement: it has

forced many couples to discuss the religious training of
their children who might otherwise have drifted along on
the heady clouds of love without facing the issue.

Early decision on the religious affiliation of the children
avoids later arguments and division within the family,
when a decision is forced. The postponed decision can be
a painful one, for the parents and for the emotional se-
curity of the children.

How do you decide the religious affiliation of the children?

By the time you are discussing this question, hopefully
you have dug deeply enough into each other's religious
beliefs so that you feel that bringing up boys and girls as
Catholics or as Episcopalians is neither a denial of your
Christian faith nor is it damaging to their religious growth.
If either partner feels he is deserting his faith by helping
to bring up his children in another church body, then the
two partners should go slowly. If there is not a very real
understanding on this point, the couple considering marriage should either spend more time in studying—or perhaps should seriously consider calling the whole thing off.
Both partners should feel that their decision on the children is in no sense a denial of their Christian heritage.
By the time you discuss the religious affiliation of your
children you should have some comprehension of the beliefs that most Christians have in common. Until you come
to such an understanding, a decision in this area could be
most difficult.

In most cases the religious affiliation of the children
probably will be somewhat obvious.

Because at the present time the Catholic church does
not recognize as "valid" a wedding in a non-Roman

church, the Catholic partner usually will want to be married in the Catholic church. Except for the rare exceptions where approval has been received for waiver of the promise on educating the children, those participating make a promise to bring up the children in the Catholic church. In probably a majority of cases this "solves" the problem.

However, as a Catholic publication of the Paulist fathers notes:

> The problem of the education of the children is the most difficult one. The self-understanding of the Catholic Church implies that the children of Catholics should normally be Catholics. It is sometimes said that it is "divine law" that the children of Catholics must be Catholics, and that, therefore, the Church could not mitigate this rule in any way. This is not true. In the past the Church has often been content with a legislation that permitted exceptions to the general rule. Even in our own day, a son of an ancient Protestant noble family of Europe, wishing to marry a Catholic girl, usually gets permission to have the children educated in the tradition of his family. If one wishes to specify how to understand the divine law in this matter, it would be better to say that in view of the self-understanding of the Catholic Church, Catholics are conscience-bound to do their best, or to do whatever is possible, to bring up their children as Catholics. They would not have to do the impossible: they would not have to threaten the unity of their home nor violate the conscience of their spouse. One can imagine situations where the Christian education of the children would be assured only if the Protestant partner tried to share his faith with them.[2]

TWO GUIDES FOR DECISION

For those cases where the decision is not obvious, we suggest two criteria which many Protestant and Catholic leaders will find unacceptable, but which we believe the realities of the situation must increasingly dictate as reasonable considerations:

1. Which partner is more active in religious observance?
2. What is the religious affiliation of the mother?

If these considerations sound less than satisfactory to church leaders who read these lines, we also have to keep in mind that present "solutions" are also less than satisfactory, and that a disturbingly high percentage of the children of a Protestant-Catholic marriage now end up in the camp of the religiously indifferent.

Studies of this are very limited and the conclusions drawn to this point may not be wholly valid, but all studies point to nearly 40 per cent of the children of a Protestant-Catholic marriage later drifting away from church affiliation. To make this figure meaningful it would have to be compared with a study of the children of those who have the same affiliation. But it seems safe to assume that the figure in the Protestant-Catholic marriage is higher, and that different approaches are needed. One is suggested in Chapter X for the churches.

For the individuals the two questions we have posed, we believe, are basic.

If one spouse is an active Catholic and the other a weak Methodist, the children probably should be raised as Catholics. If one is an active Methodist and the other a weak Catholic, the children probably should be raised as Methodists. Ideally both parents should be active in their churches, but since, as the educators say, "attitudes are caught and not taught," it is highly unlikely that a weak Catholic or a weak Methodist is going to bring up a child imbued with a strong sense of religious concern.

There is general agreement in studies which have been

made that it is difficult for a Catholic mother to bring up Protestant children or for a Protestant mother to bring up Catholic children. If all other factors make determination of the children's religious affiliation uncertain, then it seems logical on the basis of research available to suggest that the children be brought up in the church of the mother. Usually the mother plays the dominant role in rearing children and determining their religious attitudes. Under these circumstances it takes an exceedingly able and understanding mother to bring up her children in a church affiliation other than her own. One study shows the percentage of church dropouts more than double the usual rate when the mother tries to bring up children in a church other than her own. There is some evidence also that when the mother tries to bring up children in a church other than her own, the divorce rate is higher. The Michigan study mentioned earlier in the book, for example, showed the following percentages of marriages ending in divorce:

Table IX

Percentage of Marriages Ending in Divorce, Michigan Study

Both Catholic	4.4
Both Jewish	5.2
Both Protestant	6.0
Protestant-Catholic, where the Protestant became a Catholic	10.7
Protestant-Catholic, where the Catholic became a Protestant	10.6
Protestant father-Catholic mother	6.7
Catholic father-Protestant mother	20.6[3]

It is worth noting that the marriage where the father is Protestant and the mother Catholic had only a slightly higher rate of divorce than when both are Protestant, less than one percentage point difference. In this study the high divorce rate came with the Catholic husband-Protestant wife situation. This can be partially explained by the fact that a majority of divorce actions are initiated by wives rather than husbands, and Catholic wives not believing in divorce would be less likely to start such legal action. But there is rather widespread agreement among counselors and researchers that the marriage which asks the wife to bring up the children in a belief other than her own runs special dangers.

It should be added again that studies to this point are very limited. In the Catholic husband-Protestant wife situation, where the children are to be Catholic, there are many who have done it successfully. When a Protestant journal reacted unfavorably to the very limited relaxations made by Pope Paul VI in marriage regulations, it received the following letter:

> I'm a Protestant with a B.D. degree from Yale, married to a Roman Catholic. My husband and I did much searching before our marriage, but we were married in the Catholic church, and I intend to bring our children up Catholics. I agree with you that the Roman Catholic demands are wrong and unChristian. However, I certainly did not "relinquish . . . all influence over the spiritual destiny of my children." Neither did I "confer upon an institution" in which I don't believe "tyrannical power" over my children's religious education. . . .
>
> I felt when I signed the promise, and still feel, that I would be bringing up our children as Christians—in the Roman Catholic tradition although with much Protestantism thrown in. I pray that they will be good Catholics, because I think that means they'll be close to Christ, as much as if they were good Episcopalians, Presbyterians, etc. . . . To say that Protestants who make those promises are necessarily violating their Protestant principles is to make [them] feel guilt that I don't think you are justified in making them feel [and to] indicate that what is important is their faithfulness to their denominational background. Isn't what is really important their faithfulness to the church as the whole body

of Christians, and to Christ himself? Perhaps their expression of faithfulness is to show forth Christ's unity in their marriage in spite of the disunion of the churches. . . .

DOROTHY (MRS. ROBERT) McCABE
NORRISTOWN, PA.[4]

This Pennsylvania mother speaks for many. Her type of situation presents special obstacles which can be overcome. In saying that, we do not mean to lightly gloss over this type of situation, nor should a couple entering a marriage do so.

On balance, the evidence, we believe, suggests that ordinarily every couple, in determining the religious affiliation of their children, should consider both the relative degree of interest of each spouse, and the mother's affiliation.

EXPLAINING TO CHILDREN

How do you explain to children the difference in affiliation?

We don't have all the answers, for our children are ages five and two. But so far there is no problem and our five-year-old simply understands that her father goes to a different church on Sunday morning, just as he does different things from her mother during the week. And every so often the family goes to "Daddy's church," and since her grandfather and uncle are Lutheran ministers and she has seen them serving as pastors in a church service, she has some limited understanding of both religious cultures. As she and her brother grow older and ability to comprehend increases, we believe that explanations should not be difficult. Above all, we hope she will never hear anything derogatory from either of us or our relatives about either affiliation.

Most prayers (See Appendix) are thoroughly acceptable to Protestant and Catholic traditions, so prayers at
mealtime, or in the evening present no problem. For the
mealtime prayer we found that it was actually neither the
Catholic culture nor the Lutheran culture which dominated, but the television culture; a prayer our daughter
heard on a children's television program was the one she
wanted to use and it became adopted:

> God is great;
> God is good;
> Let us thank Him
> For our food.

When vacationing with her Lutheran grandparents she
learned two lines she added:

> By His love we all are fed;
> Thank You Lord for daily bread.

When that is preceded by the sign of the cross and the
words: "In the name of the Father, the Son, and the Holy
Spirit," the prayer becomes some kind of a television-
Lutheran-Catholic combination.

Because Paul has a somewhat hectic schedule that takes
him out of town a great deal, plus away for breakfast,
lunch, and dinner speaking engagements even when he is
at home, the family devotions at breakfast or dinner which
many families have are somewhat difficult to develop at
our home. Partially substituting is a good selection of religious books geared to our daughter's level; she has had
them read to her so often that she can now "read" most of
them herself. Our two-year-old now also is starting an
interest in them. A good example of this type of religious
book for children is the Arch books (for ages 3 to 11),
sold by Protestant and Catholic bookstores, which tell

biblical stories in children's language, with excellent illustrations that children and adults can appreciate. They are
very small and sell for thirty-five cents each. Another good
example is the Little People Paperbacks, about the same
price.

Both of us appreciate good music but have exceedingly
limited talents; because of our deficiencies the ecumenical
hymnal published by the Gregorian Institute of America in
the Toledo diocese does not get the use in our home it
might in many. It is titled: "Hymnal of Christian Unity."
Protestants and Catholics will find many fine hymns in it
which we all share. As a matter of fact, Protestants will
probably recognize more hymns in this Catholic book than
will most Catholics.

When Christmas approaches, our family follows another
fine Christian tradition; we have an advent wreath. Our
two-year-old will be old enough to appreciate it next year,
to help put out the candles, even though the significance
of it will largely escape him.

In a year or two when our younger child is old enough
to understand things a little more, we plan to ask a Jewish
family to our home near the feast of Hanukkah, to explain
the significance that festival has to those of the Jewish
faith. In this way we hope our children can learn not only
the meaning of the Christian faith in our home, but also
that this faith shows concern and understanding for people
who do not share your beliefs fully.

More illustrations could be used.

RELIGION IN THE HOME

Religion is primarily taught and caught in the home,
not in a church. If both of us show a concern for our faith

and how it is applied, we hope and pray—and believe—that this concern is contagious and will be passed on to our children, despite the inadequacies each of us too often show in living up to our ideals.

One danger should be stressed in all of this. In talking about what you have in common, unless it is followed or preceded by some study, the result can be a sort of spiritual baby food without much substance, for which you and your family soon lose your taste. The more you dig, the deeper your spiritual foundation will be. It will be difficult to give your children anything of value unless you personally have acquired something of substance.

When real probing is done, the Protestant-Catholic home is an unusual opportunity to train your children in Christian fundamentals—and with that teach understanding and concern for others that many an all-Catholic or all-Baptist home has a more difficult time conveying.

In summary then, these are points as far as your children are concerned:

1. The decision as to what affiliation they should have, ideally should be made before engagement, but in any event as quickly as possible.

2. If you are religiously indifferent, your children probably will be also, no matter what denominational tag you wear.

3. If the choice of their affiliation is not obvious, two factors should be considered: which spouse is more religiously active, and what is the affiliation of the mother?

4. Nothing derogatory should ever be said around the children about either partner's church.

5. Most home religious activities are things you can do in common, whether prayers, devotions, advent-wreath

ceremonies, or applying faith to life. Do these things together.

6. There is good religious literature acceptable to both religious traditions which they will enjoy.

7. A good Protestant-Catholic home presents an unusually fine opportunity to really think through the fundamentals of Christian faith and to teach understanding for the beliefs of others.

As one writer in the field notes: "Religion that is rigid and ritualistic and nothing else can destroy a family, break a marriage; but religion that is inward and real can only strengthen it."[5]

ADOPTION

One final postscript on this chapter which may be important to you in the years to come, a postscript which indicates the changing patterns. Not too many years ago if a Protestant-Catholic couple wanted to adopt a baby through an agency it was almost impossible. Today most agencies no longer retain such a barrier, unless it is a religious agency. In Illinois, for example, Catholic and Lutheran agencies continue to prefer couples where both prospective parents belong to the church of the agency; but the highly respected Illinois Children's Home and Aid Society no longer automatically disqualifies the interchurch couple.

This means that if your marriage is not blessed with children of your own, you can make a home for some who need your love and attention.

The Protestant-Catholic childless couple no longer automatically faces a future without children.

NOTES TO CHAPTER VII

1. Dr. Norman Vincent Peale, *Look,* March 22, 1955.
2. Gregory Baum, O.S.A., "Mixed Marriage—An Ecumenical Issue," *The Ecumenist,* July–August 1966.
3. Judson T. Landis, "Marriages of Mixed and Non-Mixed Religious Faiths," *American Sociological Review,* June 1949.
4. Mrs. Robert McCabe, *Christian Century,* June 22, 1966.
5. Ardis Whitman, "Children of Interfaith Marriage," *Redbook,* June 1963.

VIII
Birth Control

One of the sensitive areas which your marriage may have to face is that of the possible use of birth control pills or devices. Decisions reached should not violate the conscience of either party to a marriage, yet there are practical problems.

The official Roman Catholic position is still that the only acceptable means of birth control which does not violate natural law is the rhythm method, generally regarded as considerably less than satisfactory.

TYPES OF PROBLEMS

Here are the types of problems which ultimately you may have to face:

The two of you marry relatively young and decide that if you can have five children spaced about two years apart this would be ideal. But soon you find that the rhythm method does not work and you have three children in less than three years. Neither of you is happy with this situation. What do you do?

Your wife is in a serious automobile accident a few

weeks after your marriage. She suffers a crushed pelvis
and damage to internal organs. The doctor advises that to
attempt to have any children would be a great risk to the
health of your wife and there is a real possibility that any
child would suffer physical damage prior to birth. Is it
right to ignore what the doctor says?

Your first two children are healthy, happy, and well
adjusted, but then there are three serious miscarriages,
where the mother suffers great loss of blood and the doctors tell you that any more attempts to have children will
endanger the mother's life, or may bring into the world a
child with a serious defect. What do you do?

After four children are born the doctors inform you
that you have a malignancy. An operation appears to be
successful, but is it right to bring more children into the
world on your limited finances, with the clouds of un-
certainty hanging over your health?

These are practical cases: dozens of others could be
mentioned—and you could face any of them.

In addition to these personal situations, there is increasing evidence that, with the added medical knowledge
which civilization now has, within the next half-century
the earth will be much too heavily populated.

"Fill the earth and subdue it," was God's admonition to
early man. There are many who believe we have fulfilled
that command, and that bringing children into the world
for whom we cannot adequately provide is a disservice to
the children and to mankind.

If the Catholic spouse has some difficulties of conscience over this issue, it is to his credit, for it shows that
he does not take the leadership of his church lightly.

A change is gradually taking place within the Catholic
church on birth control with more and more cardinals and

bishops—people like Cardinals Suenens and Leger—taking the position that "natural law" does not demand that people continue to have children on an unlimited basis, that for many parents it may be more God-pleasing to have two children and take care of them well than to have ten children inadequately cared for. "The parents themselves and no one else should make the judgment about family size," according to Vatican Council II. As Father Gregory Baum, O.S.A., a theological adviser to the Vatican Council and a leader in the ecumenical movement, has noted: "With the advance of science and the growth of our awareness of our personhood, what appeared natural at one time may turn out to be, on a deeper level, against nature; and what at one time had seemed to violate the laws of nature may, after greater insight, turn out to be in harmony with it."[1]

Father Baum, director of the Center for Ecumenical Studies in Toronto, has also pointed out that the Pope has "asked" Catholics to follow past practices. Father Baum adds: "The Pope, however, did not impose this on the Catholic people. Seeing the division of the Catholic church on this issue, a strict obligation to follow the norms of the past could not be imposed. According to the Catholic tradition, whenever a moral principle is doubtful or uncertain, Catholics must follow their own informed conscience on the matter. For this reason, the priest who tells his people that they may follow their conscience in the matter of contraception does not go against the mind of the Church."[2] Conservative Catholic theologians, of course, disagree with Father Baum in this analysis.

In the magazine *Cross Currents* Catholic Bishop Francis Simons of India took a strong stand for a change in the church's position on birth control, pointing to the danger to humanity of overpopulation, and adding bluntly: "Nature seems to impose no moral obligation either to marry or, when married, to have children."[3]

The early position of the Catholic church is clear. In 1930 Pope Pius XI called use of birth control devices "criminal" and added: "No reason, however grave, may be put forward by which anything intrinsically against nature may become conformable to nature and morally good. Since, therefore, the conjugal act is destined primarily for the begetting of children, those who in exercising it deliberately frustrate its natural power and purposes, sin against nature and commit a deed which is shameful and intrinsically vicious."[4]

The Protestant stand was identical. It is often forgotten that the antibirth-control laws which some of our states had were placed on the books by Protestants, not by Catholics.

Prior to and during World War II many Protestant leaders underwent a rethinking of this issue, so that today the overwhelming Protestant position is that birth control is neither right nor wrong, of itself, but like almost anything can be used for good purposes or evil purposes.

GRADUAL CHANGE

The Catholic position has undergone a gradual change during the past ten years. The initial commission appointed by Pope Paul VI to investigate the matter was divided almost down the middle on whether birth control pills are morally acceptable. A second commission then was appointed and the as yet uncertain result appears to be a slight shifting of position, enough to satisfy some of the progressives, and not so far that those who have been preaching against it all these years are placed in an awkward position. This is not meant to imply that the decisions to be reached are primarily political in nature. Both conservatives and liberals have approached the problem prayerfully and carefully and are more concerned about reaching a God-pleasing decision than a man-pleasing one.

The gradual shift from the 1930 position of Pope Pius XI which called any use of birth control "criminal" to the current situation can hardly be denied. In February 1966 Pope Paul VI referred to birth control as "a difficulty and problem still under study," considerably milder language than that used by his predecessors. Early in 1967 Pope Paul gave cautious approval to government efforts to reduce population growth, and a few days later it was revealed in the *National Catholic Reporter* that the second papal commission was overwhelmingly in favor of a modification of the more traditional stand on birth control. Even if Pope Paul VI should simply reaffirm the traditional church stand—and some conservatives believe he may—no one expects him to do so in the strong language of Catholic documents of a few decades ago.

In Chile, where the Catholic authorities are considered to be on the liberal side, Catholics are being advised to follow their own conscience on the matter. The head of the Latin American family-planning agency is a priest. When asked at a press conference about government policies encouraging birth control use, a high-ranking Catholic priest of Chile, Msgr. Hernan Larrain, said: "For Catholics, there is liberty to follow conscience." Church authorities in Chile have made it clear that while the pills are deemed unobjectionable, the intra-uterine devices are not considered a morally acceptable birth control device because they may be abortive.

In the United States the more liberal Catholic press generally supports a change in the church position on the morality of the use of birth control pills, and other birth control devices. Even the conservative Catholic periodicals are considerably more moderate in their position than they once were.

In one of the conservative journals the following question was asked:

> When a married couple has in conscience decided that the Church teaching, or position on birth control is WRONG, may they continue to receive Communion? Are they obligated to mention this decision to a confessor?
>
> By birth control I refer to both mechanical means and the pill. The assumption is that pills are esthetically preferable. But, if necessary, mechanical devices will be used. In other words, they repudiate the whole position of the Church as being wrong, unrealistic, unsound, etc. Yet they have no desire to "leave the Church formally. The Church is just wrong, that's all."

In answer the priest-columnist says that if "the couple is sincerely convinced that they are acting rightly—then they could in good conscience continue to receive Communion. And they would be obligated to mention their decision to a confessor only in the measure that they might have doubts about it." He then went on to add: "It does not seem possible that a Catholic who accepts the teaching authority of the Church in matters of morality could hold mechanical methods of birth control to be legitimate. . . . With regard to the pill, the position of the Church is less firmly established."[5]

Several of the limited studies which have been made indicate that the percentage of Catholics using birth control pills is almost as great as the rest of the population. The 1966 fifth annual Notre Dame Conference on Population released a study showing that a majority of Roman Catholic wives between the ages of 19 and 39 no longer conform to traditional church doctrine in the matter of birth control. A study in Columbia, released by the Catholic church in that country, showed that less than 3 per cent of the population was even aware that the Catholic church took a stand on the issue of birth control. To be more meaningful, that percentage figure would have to be related to other data, but it does indicate a changing church scene.

All of this may not solve your particular problem. But it is safe to say that because of changing attitudes, birth control is less of a problem in a Protestant-Catholic marriage than it once was.

To those who feel they cannot in good conscience use the birth control pills, or other devices, the two options which remain are the rhythm method of birth control and abstinence. Because of the many problems inherent in abstaining from the sexual act, the latter does not seem to be a practical answer for the ordinary couple; it is an answer fraught with great danger to the marriage.

Marriage generally should not be planned as childless; if one partner has a family history of a particular severe disease or mutation, the answer may be that your children should come through adoption. But children are almost essential to family completeness; nieces and nephews are a poor substitute.

Whatever your situation, circumstances may force a realistic appraisal of the possible use of birth control.

No one's conscience should be violated.

But the issue should not be avoided.

NOTES TO CHAPTER VIII

1. Gregory Baum, O.S.A., quoted in the *National Catholic Reporter,* May 25, 1966.
2. Gregory Baum, O.S.A., *National Catholic Reporter,* April 20, 1966, quoting from the Toronto *Globe.*
3. Bishop Francis Simons, *Cross Currents,* quoted in *National Catholic Reporter,* December 14, 1966.
4. Pope Pius XI, Encyclical on Christian Marriage, 1930.
5. *Our Sunday Visitor,* March 20, 1966.

IX

Be Willing to Help

Once you have crossed the barrier of a Protestant-Catholic marriage you will be surprised to learn how many others have done the same. Statistics from this book or any source are not as meaningful as suddenly learning that a cousin of yours also married a Baptist or a Catholic, that the couple just two doors away has a Protestant-Catholic marriage.

Because so much of the material which is available to the concerned couple contemplating a Protestant-Catholic marriage is negative and unhelpful, you may have the opportunity to be of some positive assistance to others from time to time. When that opportunity presents itself, we hope you will speak frankly to your friends. They will not expect professional counseling from you, but you may actually be in a position to give better advice than those more accustomed to counseling who all their lives have heard only the negative aspects of such a marriage.

Episcopal Bishop James A. Pike has offered advice to those wanting to help a couple considering a Protestant-

Catholic marriage. Among his suggestions are the following:

1. At no point should the impression be given that it doesn't matter what people believe.
2. Don't get bogged down in minor points.
3. Be fair.
4. Encourage questions.
5. Talk to both parties at once.[1]

These are good points, but should not necessarily be followed rigidly. The best discussions are unstructured and informal. Encourage your friends to talk to others also about their decision. But if you speak to them frankly and sympathetically, they will be grateful.

The fifth point, talking to both parties at once, is probably one the pastor or priest or person accustomed to more formal counseling can follow easily. Our experience is that ordinarily the Protestant-Catholic couple is approached for advice by only one of the two parties involved. This does not make Bishop Pike's point any less valid; ideally we believe he is right and the married couple can suggest to the person who first approaches them that the two contemplating marriage should come over some evening for a cup of coffee and together all four of you can discuss the matter.

The suggestion that you make sure not to give the impression that it does not matter what people believe is particularly important. The couple contemplating a Protestant-Catholic marriage is sometimes encouraged by the indifference of friends. "It once made a difference what people believed, but today that's not important," they advise. What people believe continues to be most important—and this the concerned couple should learn, but learn in perspective. If two Baptists marry and one believes that his

Christian faith demands that he show love and concern for the Negro and the other believes the Negro is inferior and that he must help "keep the Negro in his place," obviously they face a problem. It does make a difference what each believes; one happens to be right, the other wrong.

In the case of this Baptist couple their attitude toward the Negro and their division may well be much greater than that in a Protestant-Catholic marriage and may suggest more deep-seated differences which divide them. What people believe is important, and when counseling with a couple considering marriage you should ask them to learn what each really believes. If the Catholic harbors deep-seated antagonisms toward Protestants, or the Protestant harbors deep-seated antagonisms toward Catholics, the time to learn this is not after marriage but before. How will their beliefs affect an issue like birth control? How do they plan to bring up their children? Does this violate the conscience of either party? Here again, your practical experience can be most helpful to the couple considering the move you have made.

HELPING OTHERS UNDERSTAND

Your marriage also will be an opportunity to help your friends and relatives be a little more understanding of "the other side." Your home should be a good place for Protestants and Catholics to meet informally over a cup of coffee or a dinner, expressing their doubts and concerns and in the process learning how much they have in common.

As one writer notes: "Intermarriage between young people of different religious ancestry and traditions may cause little difficulty and lead to many positive values if both parties are tolerant in religious outlook. The very fact of difference may, under these circumstances, enrich their love and family life. Such a marriage can mean enlarged horizons. It has implications for better intergroup relations and unity in the democratic community."[2]

Within your own church organizations you will occasionally be asked about a Protestant or Catholic position because it is known that you have a spouse of another affiliation. At a confraternity meeting Jeanne sometimes points out the Lutheran position on a matter, and at a Lutheran meeting Paul is sometimes asked about the Catholic attitude toward a certain thing.

This ability to help others facing a Protestant-Catholic marriage and the chance to promote understanding should not become reasons or excuses for a Protestant-Catholic marriage; but they are special opportunities such a marriage presents.

Here is an actual example of what is happening:

In New York City, Jack, a Roman Catholic, and Karen, a Lutheran, both active in their churches, decided to get married. They talked it over with a Jesuit priest whom they both knew, and among other things he suggested that they should discuss the matter with the Lutheran pastor. He also indicated that they should attend some Lutheran and Catholic services together before marriage. They did—including celebrating Holy Communion together in both churches without the approval of either the Catholic priest or Lutheran pastor; but Jack and Karen felt the two churches believe in the Real Presence and saw no reason not to commune together. After counseling with both ministers and priests they were married in the Catholic church. The church bulletin of the Lutheran parish noted: "Jack _____and Karen_____will be married Sunday.

Both have celebrated with us, and Karen is a regular part of our community. Jack is a Roman Catholic, but they both have exciting plans for a Christian home and family. They will be married at_____[the Catholic church], with Pastor_____[the Lutheran minister] taking part in the ceremony."

It is difficult to believe that either the Lutheran or Catholic parish could help but come away with a little more understanding, where priests and ministers and those involved worked together carefully.

News of this kind of incident needs to be circulated much more—and those involved in a Protestant-Catholic marriage are just the ones to spread this good and helpful news.

The hope once existed that Christian unity would be promoted by "conversion"; but statistics show that there is so much cross-traffic in church affiliations that those who wish to bring about greater Christian unity no longer consider "conversion" a means toward that end.

While ultimate Christian unity is beyond the lifetime of anyone reading these lines, Christian understanding and cooperation which must precede unity is becoming more of a reality.

The growing number of Protestant-Catholic marriages may become a major factor in promoting more cooperation and understanding.

NOTES TO CHAPTER IX

1. James A. Pike, *If You Marry Outside Your Faith* (New York: Harper and Brothers, 1954), pp. 181–84.
2. Algernon D. Black, *If I Marry Outside My Religion* (New York: Public Affairs Committee, 1954), p. 26.

X

A Postscript to the Churches

Primarily this chapter is for the counselor and church leader who has shown an interest and concern in this problem area, and who is willing to listen to a few unorthodox approaches.

This final chapter is intended for the couple involved in a Protestant-Catholic marriage to the extent that they find themselves in positions of influence and leadership within their respective churches.

SUGGESTIONS FOR IMPROVEMENT

If the following suggestions were to be followed, the climate could improve for those who may be experiencing some very difficult decisions:

1. *Make the partner to such a marriage continue to feel welcome in your church.*

If a Protestant marries in a Catholic church, or a Catholic marries in a Protestant church, there are many willing and eager to condemn the person. Until recently excom-

munication was a common practice for this breech in the
Catholic church, also in some Protestant churches. More
subtle but just as effective is to view the offender as someone who somehow should not share in the joys and re-
sponsibilities of Christian worship and fellowship; the
"cold shoulder" is quickly felt. Obviously this accomplishes
nothing. The Protestant-Catholic marriage can be a sign
of spiritual weakness—although by no means is that necessarily the case; but if it is, then the person needs to be
lifted up, not pushed down. To what extent are those in a
Protestant-Catholic marriage encouraged to be involved in
the activities of your parish?

2. *Don't overstress theological niceties as barriers when
actually they have little meaning to most laymen.*

The most obvious example is the admonition in virtually all books on the subject that there is a very fundamen-
tal and basic cleavage between Protestants and Catholics in
their view of marriage. The Catholic views marriage as a
sacrament, while the Protestant views marriage as a cove-
nant between man and God, and man and man, mysteri-
ously designed by God to which He gives His special bless-
ing. There yet remains a difference, but to most laymen
the difference between the two positions is much the same
as the ancient argument about how many angels could
stand on the head of a pin. The difference that does exist
does not drastically alter the nature of the marriage.

3. *The Protestant-Catholic marriage should not be a
battleground for the churches.*

There is little excuse anywhere for the old-fashioned
religious wars which have been waged in communities all

over the world between Protestants and Catholics—and there is even less excuse for people to divide families in such a way, ironically and tragically doing it in the name of Christianity. The New Testament refers to those who kill Christians and believe they are serving God; within the Christian church there are those who kill marriages and do it in the name of God. This type of blasphemous conduct should be considered as out-of-bounds for a clergyman or church leader as stealing from the collection plate—and if you were to choose between the two, the lesser sin would appear to be stealing from the collection plate. A marriage, sanctified by God, is no place for churches to carry out their petty wars.

4. *When a Protestant-Catholic marriage does occur, the Protestant pastor and Catholic priest should get together to discuss how they can best help the couple.*

Here is a practical place where the ecumenical movement can be put to work. If a Baptist boy marries a Catholic girl, there is no reason why the Baptist minister and Catholic priest should not get together to discuss how they can mutually best help this couple. The simple fact that they get together to discuss the matter says something to the couple involved, and to the community. This suggestion is neither novel nor impractical, and has been put forward by several Protestant and Catholic journals. One book puts the case well: "The only plausible solution to the mixed marriage dilemma is joint pastoral counseling by both priest and minister. Together they can help the couple to understand the common elements of their religious beliefs, as well as those areas in which they are divided. Such a step would also be a form of common

Christian mission to the innocent victims of ecclesiastical divisions. . . . Their pastoral guides must explain that their common commitment to Jesus Christ, sealed by Christian baptism, unites them more effectively than any doctrinal difference may divide them."[1] *Commonweal,* a Catholic publication, has suggested that "ecumenical groups of priests and ministers who would cooperatively counsel couples in mixed marriage" be formed. Having outside groups of clergy may be desirable for instances when the two clergymen most directly involved do not get together, perhaps because of attitudes and personalities. But ideally, where the minister and priest of the couple can get together, this would appear to be the better approach.

5. *Once a Protestant-Catholic marriage takes place, look for practical ways for the respective churches to cooperate.*

The counseling suggested prior to marriage sometimes needs to take place after marriage on a cooperative basis.

A Catholic publication makes one excellent suggestion for cooperation: "The sacrament of Baptism should unite divided Christians. However, law may make of it another source of division. The child is not a pawn nor the church a club. Because a Lutheran and a Roman Catholic can be one in Jesus Christ, the laws of both churches should make it possible for their children's baptisms in one church to be entered upon the register of the other church. The event of such baptisms could unite the churches in a common joy in spite of their divisions."[2]

Churches should cooperate where possible now, and where changes in church law can make possible a further working together without compromising basic doctrines, those changes should take place.

6. *Protestants must view a little more critically the stand taken by some of their leaders regarding the permanency of marriage.*

It is little wonder that Catholics view with amazement and disfavor the practice of some Protestant clergy who officiate with the solemn words, "What God hath joined together, let no man put asunder"—and then intone these words to marry the same person three times ("until death do us part"), two living, discarded spouses the not-too-silent evidence of some loose practices. A *Christian Century* (Protestant) article notes:

> African Christian leaders, wrestling with their own puzzle of polygamy, point out that some of the older churches are willing to bless what amounts to the same practice, only on a consecutive basis. Have they a point?
>
> A firm and consistent stand on indissolubility gives support to a couple whose original intention was to enter a permanent union. Protestant softness on divorce may fall short of sustaining family solidarity through marital crises which could be weathered if the spiritual defenses were stronger. Middle-aged Catholic couples sometimes express gratitude for the scaffolding which held them secure through periods of fatigue, boredom, turmoil, and brought them to maturity more fully one. "Had divorce been an alternative, there were times we might have taken it," a Catholic woman says honestly.
>
> Further probing of the meaning of marriage is needed throughout the entire Christian church.[3]

7. *Catholics must view with new perspective rules which may violate someone's conscience and rules which do not respect a marriage which takes place outside the Catholic church.*

Under the March 1966 decree of Pope Paul VI, a Catholic is no longer excommunicated automatically for being married in a non-Catholic Christian church. This is certainly a small step in the right direction. But serious— and indefensible—barriers yet remain. A baptism in a Lutheran church is recognized by the Catholic church; a marriage in a Lutheran church between a Catholic and a Lutheran is not recognized as valid. As the Jesuit publication *America* notes: "Both Christian unity and Christian marriage stand to gain from continuing concern for the validity of all marriages among Christians."[4] Even the official publication of a conservative Catholic diocese editorially criticized the papal decree of March 1966 for not going further, characterizing the document as "an enigma" and "unecumenical."[5] A Catholic book notes: "The instruction [of March 1966] subordinates the welfare of the married couple to the welfare of the Catholic party. Even though there are a few positive points, the instruction does not change the essentially negative character of previous legislation."[6]

In an interview in the German news magazine *Der Spiegel* the prominent Catholic theologian, Fathers Hans Kueng, proposed two steps which would ease considerably the friction between Catholics and Protestants and would lessen the burden some Protestant-Catholic marriages face. His suggestion: that "marriage in non-Catholic churches should be recognized as valid" and that "the question of baptism and training for children born from a mixed marriage should be left entirely to parents."[7] He said that the result of the second proposal would be that the parent with the stronger religious beliefs would ordinarily prevail about the child's religious upbringing.

Father Kueng's second point would take care of the case where the active Episcopalian girl marries a weak Catholic boy. Under present Catholic regulations, if the wedding takes place before a Catholic priest and is "valid," the children theoretically must be brought up as Catholics —and studies indicate that under these circumstances they may grow up as nothing.

Commonweal (Catholic) has editorially commented:

> Now that a new era is upon the Church, an era marked by a fresh sensitivity to the non-Catholic conscience, the present laws are patently anachronistic. They hearken back to that period when the impersonal rights of truth were held to take precedence over every other consideration, when the principle that "error has no rights" was thought to be the final word on the claims of the non-Catholic conscience. That period has, happily, just about passed in the Church-State arena; it is now time that some of the same insights which brought it to a close be applied to the church's marriage legislation.[8]

Such a change also follows the spirit of Vatican II and is supported by these words from the Decree on the Apostolate of the Laity: "It has always been the duty of Christian couples, but today it is the supreme task of their apostolate, to manifest and prove by their own way of life the unbreakable and sacred character of the marriage bond, to affirm vigorously the right and duty of parents and guardians to educate children in a Christian manner, and to defend the dignity and lawful independence of the family." The Declaration on Christian Education of the same Vatican Council notes: "Parents must be acknowledged as the first and foremost educators of their children."

Yet despite the recognition of the independence of the family, of the primary obligation of parents as educators, and a new spirit of communion among all Christian churches, some of the present regulations of the Catholic church on the validity of marriage and the religious affiliation of the children stand as tragic monuments to part of an unhappy and recent past. (It is interesting to note that until 1908 most Catholic marriages before a minister or even a justice of the peace were considered valid.)

An extreme example of the awkwardness of the present regulations is cited by Msgr. J. D. Conway: "Suppose I am called to see a poor man dying with cancer who has been married out of the Church and now wishes the marriage to be made valid so that he can receive the last sacraments. I must require that he sign promises that all children to be born of his new Catholic marriage will be baptized and educated in the Church, and I must get his grieving wife to promise that she will not interfere with his carrying out a promise which in a few days he will be able to accomplish only from heaven. And if her conscience will not permit her to make this promise I must send the case to Rome, with hope of receiving a reply a year after the funeral."[9]

Less important needed changes in church law could be cited.

A ridiculous extreme that still applies in some Catholic dioceses is the prohibition against the Protestant spouse being buried next to his Catholic partner in a Catholic cemetery. This fortunately is no longer the case in most areas, but where it still is the rule of the diocese, it is one of those little, ridiculous, irksome things which Protestants and Catholics understandably and rightfully find objectionable. A good example of the proper attitude is that taken in 1966 by the Winona, Minnesota, diocese. The Religious News Service reported that a diocesan directive urged that "cemeteries established in the future should be for all people, without any distinction between Catholic and non-Catholic."

8. *The churches should look to the Protestant-Catholic marriage as a symbol of the church itself.*

Like the church, the Protestant-Catholic couple is united with Christ—yet like the church it is also divided. The couple must be told that what unites them is much greater than what divides them, just as the church must recognize this about its own division.

In the process of strengthening such an intrafaith marriage, the church strengthens itself and approaches a little more closely the type of unity for which too many religious leaders seem willing to pray, but for which they too often are unwilling to take practical steps.

The Protestant-Catholic marriage is one of those practical opportunities present in almost every parish.

In 1964 an Episcopal priest and a Roman Catholic priest officiated at a wedding of a couple in Missouri. It was one of the first such occurrences within the United States and brought a brief flurry of newspaper and magazine attention. The Episcopal priest involved sent a letter to the *Christian Century* which should be required reading for all Protestant and Catholic leaders:

> Sir: Since the marriage of Susan Ekberg and Patrick Barker has received attention in the *Century,* it occurred to Bishop George L. Cadigan of the diocese of Missouri [that I should] write you concerning some of the background of the event, since I was the participating Episcopal priest, pastor to the bride and her family. The beginning was not extraordinary: After a decent courtship, two sensitive and intelligent young people decided to marry. The man was a Roman Catholic, the woman an Episcopalian. Both seemed to have a rather satisfying attachment to their re-

spective churches and an adequate understanding of the gospel. Both were naive in regard to the existing schisms within the Christian church, having been blinded by the informal graciousness they had experienced between Roman Catholics and Episcopalians, together with the natural distaste we all have for that which is confusing, irrational and unpleasant.

As they found their way into the ecclesiastical hideouts of these two great churches, they became increasingly and painfully aware of the discrepancy between what the churches say about brotherhood in Christ and the manner in which ecclesiastical institutions often find themselves compelled to behave for their own aggrandizement. Their experience was, to say the least, not uncommon.

To abandon their churches lightly and marry before the civil authority by reason of this internecine strife would raise intolerable questions about their ability to be serious about anything, including marriage; on the other hand, their ecclesiastical allegiances could not neutralize their love for one another. In other terms, they were in the midst of a very serious crisis in identity, and as this is a constant plague to all of us it is well that we recognize it as such.

It was to this problem that the two families along with Fr. Leonard Jackson, O.S.B., Cardinal Ritter, Bishop Cadigan and I addressed ourselves. We are grateful to have been spared the necessity to labor the obvious; neither church was able to change its commitments to itself. Should we then seek to leave our mark on this affair by driving the wedge between us even more deeply in the name of institutional integrity? We felt that neither church had any reason to act defensively, as whatever integrity either of us had came from healing not wounding.

Could not, then, in the midst of this separation, some small sign be given which indicated our conviction that it is better to be together than apart? The wedding, in a Roman church, using the Book of Common Prayer, with an Episcopal and Roman priest equally responsible as officiants, was the best we could do. Accepting the things we could not change, we did our best to help Susan remain

Susan, Patrick to remain Patrick, and the two of them to become man and wife.

Questions have been raised about who won and who lost. I think I speak for all directly concerned when I say that I hope both churches lost some pride and passion and both gained some dignity; that Susan and Patrick lost their naivete and found themselves; and that all of us realized that we can lose ourselves in an ancient and honorable institution in order to find a way to justify our sinfulness. My fear is not that we lost to the Romans, but that we both lost two fine young people because of our gnatty preoccupations.

If ecumenicity is that which emerges in spite of the hard and uncompromising, if it is an improbable and perplexing brotherhood which restores one's faith in the power of God to redeem a situation which has all the earmarks of being unredeemable, then our small band bears witness to having been briefly caught in an ecumenical experience, modest though it was.[10]

> CLAUDIUS MILLER, III
> Church of the Good Shepherd
> St. Louis, Missouri

Whatever the particular methods of reconciliation used, it is patently imperative that the Protestant-Catholic marriage must be abandoned as the battleground for Christian churches. If the churches see the increasingly frequent Protestant-Catholic marriage not as a monster to be feared, but as an opportunity to provide help to individuals and to heal the wounds of Christendom, all of us will be richer.

NOTES TO CHAPTER X

1. William J. Sullivan, C.S.P., *Mixed Marriage* (St. Meinrad, Ind.: Abbey Press, 1966), pp. 12–13.
2. *Ibid.*, p. 14.
3. Elsie Gibson, "Dialogue on Marriage," *Christian Century,* March 10, 1956.

4. "Marriage, Mixed and Invalid," editorial in *America,* February 12, 1966.
5. *Western Catholic,* April 17, 1966.
6. Sullivan, *op. cit.,* p. 7.
7. Father Hans Kueng, in *Der Spiegel,* quoted in *Western Catholic,* February 2, 1966.
8. *Commonweal,* March 5, 1965.
9. Msgr. J. D. Conway, *Mixed Marriage,* op. cit., p. 54.
10. Rev. Claudius Miller, III, *Christian Century,* December 9, 1964.

Appendix

Prayers Acceptable to Protestants and Catholics

In addition to the Lord's Prayer, and the Apostle's and Nicene Creeds, which are held in common by both Protestants and Catholics, most prayers are completely acceptable to both; those with objectionable features to either party can be easily spotted and obviously should be avoided for common use. A few of literally thousands of prayers which could have been chosen are in this appendix. Wording for some of them differs slightly, depending on the particular translations used; those listed here are acceptable to both traditions, in some instances a Catholic translation is used, and in some a Protestant translation.

THE LORD'S PRAYER

The two versions differ slightly, Protestants adding a few words at the end of the older and more traditional prayer. There is no theological problem here since the wording is acceptable to both Protestants and Catholics. The natural solution is to use the version which the children will be using. If they are to be reared as Catholic, use the Catholic version; if they are to be reared as Protestants, use the Protestant version.

TABLE PRAYER

A Catholic frequently begins a table prayer or any other prayer by making the sign of the cross with his hand, and says: "In the name of the Father, the Son, and the Holy Spirit." This custom is also followed by some Episcopalians and Lutherans. Luther recommended that those who subscribed to his Reformation principles continue the use of the sign of the cross, but most Protestants do not use it today. The most commonly used Catholic table prayer:

> Bless us, O Lord,
> And these Thy gifts
> Which we are about to receive
> From Thy bounty
> Through Christ our Lord.
>   Amen

This is, of course, acceptable to Protestants. The following widely used Protestant table prayer is acceptable to Catholics:

> Come, Lord Jesus,
> Be our guest
> And let this food
> To us be blessed.
>   Amen

Many people also have a prayer at the close of a meal, and the most commonly used Protestant and Catholic prayer is almost identical.

NIGHT PRAYERS FOR CHILDREN

Some variety in these prayers is desirable, so that it does not become entirely a matter of habit. Part of the prayer for the little ones can include: "God bless Grandma and Aunt Susie" and anyone else the child thinks of—which may include the neighbor's dog or some inanimate objects.

The Lord's Prayer is an obvious choice for a night prayer, and the following is widely used:

> Now I lay me down to sleep;
> I pray the Lord my soul to keep;
> If I should die before I wake.
> I pray the Lord my soul to take.

There are some who object to this prayer on theological grounds or as frightening children, and a variety of word changes is available for those who would prefer something else.

INFORMAL PRAYERS

Prayers are not only words handed down to us by our Christian predecessors and leaders of today, but needs which we feel and express from day to day, in language which is imperfect but beautiful. These informal, imperfect, beautiful prayers should also be cultivated.

Prayer of St. Francis of Assisi

> Lord, make me an instrument of Your peace.
> Where there is hatred, let me sow love;
> Where there is injury, pardon;
> Where there is doubt, faith;

Where there is despair, hope;
Where there is darkness, light;
And where there is sadness, joy.
O Divine Master,
Grant that I may not so much seek to be
    consoled as to console;
To be understood as to understand;
To be loved as to love,
For it is in giving that we receive;
It is in pardoning that we are pardoned;
And it is in dying that we are born to eternal
    life.

Morning Prayer of Martin Luther

I thank You, my heavenly Father, through Jesus
Christ, Your dear Son, that You have kept me this
night from all harm and danger; and I pray that
You would keep me this day also from sin and
every evil, that all my doings and life may please
You. For into Your hands I commend myself, my
body and soul and all things. Let Your holy angels
be with me, that the wicked foe may have no power
over me. Amen.

PRAYER FOR FORGIVENESS

O almighty God, give me grace to approach You with a
repenting and believing heart. I confess that I have sinned
against You in thought, word, and deed, and that I am not
worthy to be called Your child; yet, in mercy keep me as
Your child. Give me true repentance, and forgive me all my
sins; through Jesus Christ, my Lord.

                                                    Amen

PRAYER AFTER HOLY COMMUNION AND OTHER OCCASIONS

Grant, O Lord, that every moment of this day, in all my
dealings with others, I may keep in mind Your words: "What-
soever you do to one of them you do it unto Me." Grant that
I may regulate all my dealings with others according to Your
command: "Love one another as I have loved you."

PRAYER FOR TODAY

For those who suffer oppression because of the color of their
    skin;
For those who suffer because they are Jewish;
For the millions who go to bed hungry each night;
For the millions who cannot read and write;
For the mentally ill and the mentally retarded;
For those who are born out of wedlock;
For those in prison;
For those in need of help in my community;
For those who suffer the illness of hatred;
For the sick and the dying;
For the leadership of all Christian churches;
For those who worship You in different churches;
For all of these we pray Your blessings.
Give us the vision to see where we can help,
And the courage and willingness to do so.

Amen

PRAYER FOR OUR MARRIAGE

For all that unites us, we thank You;
For the opportunity to serve You in our respective churches,
    We thank You:
For the chance to work together to help men in need, we
    thank You;
For all united in marriage, we ask Your blessings;
For our children, we ask Your blessings;

For our parents, and relatives, we ask Your blessings;
Give us the vision to see need more clearly;
Give us the desire to serve with more dedication;
Give us the love to understand and tolerate difference;
O Christ, the Lamb of God, have mercy upon us;
O Christ, the Lamb of God, have mercy upon us;
O Christ, the Lamb of God, grant us Your peace.

                                                              Amen